MW01000572

# SOCIAL MEDIA IS BULLSHIT

# SOCIAL

## MEDIA

### IS

# BULLSHIT

## B. J. Mendelson

ST. MARTIN'S PRESS 🐾 NEW YORK

www.stmartins.com

Design by Steven Seighman

ISBN 978-1-250-00295-2 (hardcover)
ISBN 978-1-250-01750-5 (e-book)

First Edition: September 2012

10   9   8   7   6   5   4   3   2   1

*To Amanda:*
*I think you said it best, "If only we had known sooner, we would have done nothing different."*

# CONTENTS

*By the way, if anyone here is in advertising or marketing . . . kill yourself.*
—Bill Hicks, comedian and social critic

# AN INTRODUCTION: BULLSHIT 101

## CHAPTER ONE

# OUR TERRIBLE, HORRIBLE, NO GOOD, VERY BAD WEB SITE

---

**MY FIRST WEB SITE** nearly got me killed. I was building it using a Bondi blue G3 iMac that my dad brought home from work. At the time, I didn't know HTML, or that I could have just used GeoCities.[1] The best I could do was use Microsoft Word and save things as an .html file. I got as far as creating a single page with a black background, bright red text, and an animated GIF of a spinning globe on it. Cutting-edge stuff for the fall of 1998, my sophomore year in high school.

During a meeting of the Computer Club, I showed my friend, Whitey[2], the Web site I was working on. Whitey had bragged for weeks about the traffic his tribute Web site for *The Simpsons* was getting. Knowing I wanted to share my alleged wit with the world, Whitey told me the Web could help me find an audience, but then declared my current efforts to be a failure. He volunteered to build me a "more respectable Web site." We called the new Web site "The Island" because of my obsession with the New York Islanders, a team that embodies mediocrity. My goal with this new Web site was to document the stupid things that came out of my mouth, which I kept in a notebook (a practice

I continue to this day and recommend you follow. Not just for jokes, but anything. If you don't write it down, it'll be gone forever). Whitey didn't find any of that stuff funny, though, so he suggested we brainstorm something else we could publish.

The next time I came to his house, we got to talking about how much we hated life at Monroe-Woodbury Senior High School. We were both picked on relentlessly. Whitey was teased for being a computer nerd, back when that warranted a wedgie and not a hundred million dollars in venture capital. And me? When you run for class president and lose every year since the sixth grade, the whole school thinks you're a loser, and you've got the votes to prove it. To help blow off some steam, Whitey suggested we create a Web site where we mock our school and everyone in it. He would do the coding, and I would do the content—most of which consisted of audio files, each featuring a rant about a student we didn't like. We had a bunch of other things on there, too, but the highlight was "The Top 50 Assholes Who Go to Monroe-Woodbury Senior High School." The top fifty was a list I built and maintained by going through old yearbooks and identifying people who had picked on Whitey and I. The idea was that we would then rank those people based on how big of a dick they were that particular week.

At first, The Island only received a few hits a day. Then Whitey's friend, Brian Egan, passed the link on to some of his friends through AOL Instant Messenger, saying, "look at what Whitey made!" Word got around, and suddenly we were hit with something ridiculous like twenty-bazillion hits an hour. The Island had "gone viral."[3] To avoid our parents discovering the Web site, we kept our names off it. Whitey also took the added step of having one his friends host it on a private server . . . a server that soon crashed under the weight of all that traffic. Unfortunately, it didn't crash fast enough to keep our classmates from printing "The Top 50 Assholes Who Go to Monroe-Woodbury

Senior High School" and circulating it around school under the title of "Whitey's Death List."

When The Island came back, we were shocked to find that most people loved it, so much so that the audio files I did were recorded onto cassette tapes and passed around school like an early Metallica bootleg. A lot of people didn't talk to me back then, hence the sustained electoral failure, so at first no one knew of my involvement. They thought it was all Whitey's idea, and out of fear, I didn't persuade them otherwise. But when our classmates matched my voice with the rants, a weird thing happened. They kept harassing Whitey for being a computer nerd, but aside from the football team—who now wanted to kill me—everyone else wanted to be my friend. The Island got me the attention I was looking for.

# CHAPTER TWO
# ASTONISHING TALES OF MEDIOCRITY

**DESPITE HAVING AN** underwhelming C average after four years of high school, I told my dad the only college I would go to was NYU, and that I wouldn't apply elsewhere because "other colleges were bullshit." Knowing I wouldn't get into my school of choice, Dad filled out an application for me to attend Alfred State College. In the fall of 2001, I arrived at Alfred with a chip on my shoulder. Thanks to The Island's success, I learned that if you do something interesting, the people who normally ignored you would start paying attention to what you're doing. So, the behavior that got me rewarded my last three years of high school continued into my first year of college.

That is, until I received a lifetime ban from WETD[1], Alfred State College's radio station, and alienated everyone on campus. I didn't know it at the time, but that ban was a blessing in disguise. After The Island was deleted, I put on hold my ambition to show the world how funny I thought I was. People in high school found me amusing, and that was good enough. And considering the number of near beatings

Whitey received from the football team, I didn't want to push my luck. But Alfred State College can affectionately be described as a "Suitcase Campus." Everyone went home on the weekend, and the school is located in a tiny town in the broke and undeveloped wilderness of New York's Southern Tier. Lake Wobegon it ain't. Without money, a car, or people who *didn't* want to see me die in a circus disaster, the Web was my last refuge. In February 2002, one month after my lifetime ban from WETD went into effect, I went back to posting my poorly thought-out grammatical holocausts online.

After a year of mediocrity and spelling errors, I had a long string of humor columns go viral, starting with "The Universal Break-Up Card" in February 2003. After that, I built a name for myself with columns like "I Hate Captain Planet" and "What Would the Hulk Do?" to similar success and started writing for other people. Beginning with popular adult film star, Joanna Angel, in 2004, I worked my way up to a nationally published music magazine, and then got a college survival column syndicated to over eight hundred college newspapers through CBS College Sports. From there, I contributed to a number of outlets including The Huffington Post, Forbes, Mashable, MTV's O Music Awards, the Eisner-nominated ComicsAlliance, and CNN.

## JOURNEY INTO MYSTERY (AND MARKETING)

With the experience I gained using the Web to promote my columns, people started e-mailing me for advice on how to market themselves and their products on the Web. I never wanted to be a marketer, and at first I was reluctant to help. But college is expensive, and I needed money to impress girls who had no intention of sleeping with me. So, I caved and picked up some clients and started to do marketing for them, charging only enough to pay for textbooks. I promoted the bands whose events I also booked. Then I moved on to working with small businesses, and authors like former University of Pennsylvania professor Dr. Andrew Shatté. In 2007, I worked for *The Edge with Jake Sasseville*, a syndicated television show that aired in forty million homes on ABC affiliates, and in 2010, I helped promote Colonel John Folsom and his not-for-profit Wounded Warriors Family Support, with a national outreach campaign called "The High Five Tour." During that time I also did some work with Ford, Overstock.com, Sprint, Dunkin' Donuts, Microsoft (via Crispin Porter + Bogusky), and Sears (via Ogilvy & Mather).

But, I don't claim to be a marketing prodigy. I had about as many marketing successes as I did sexual escapades during college: zero.

In 2007, frustrated by the lack of results, I started listening to what other marketers were saying about the Web, and parroted it to my clients. I knew whatever I was doing wasn't working, so when I started taking on clients full-time, I used an old psychological trick I learned from Professor William Laubert at Alfred State College: People bring their experiences with you to the meeting, and they connect it to the idea you're proposing.[2] You could have the best idea in the world, but if people don't like you, don't trust you, or don't know you, they're not going to consider it. However, if you cite what someone else is saying, someone they might have heard of, that lends the idea more credibility. "Another way to look at it," Laubert added, "would be to think of the person as looking at you with blue tinted sunglasses (their previous experiences are 'coloring' the way that they perceive you). By using other sources that the audience finds credible, it's sort of like having them put on a different colored pair of glasses—you haven't changed but the way the audience perceives you changes. Before you appeared sort of blue, but now you look green."[3]

Using this trick worked well to attract clients, so I continued doing it, name-dropping marketers with a public profile—people like Gary Vaynerchuk, Seth Godin, and Chris Brogan.

You know what the problem with that is? Everything the professional marketers say makes sense on paper, but little of it actually works in practice.

# CHAPTER THREE
## "I WROTE THIS BOOK FOR PEPSI"

**THERE ARE MANY** factors involving the mostly fictional world of marketing, and they're all dependent on your specific set of circumstances. So, there's no way for me—or anyone—to give you an effective marketing strategy that's also going to work for everyone else. If you do what I used to and repeat what the professional marketers say, that may score you some points in attracting clients, but it'll do nothing to keep their business. The best any marketing author can do, therefore, is give you the basics and tell you what they've learned. The rest is up to you.

Unfortunately, none of them do this. What they do is hand out bad advice based on little evidence, and then sprinkle some buzzwords and useless theory on top for good measure.[1] And when they're done, they try to upsell you on their other services. The blatant upselling is most obvious when the author will spend the entire book explaining why you should use something, but then never tell you how. Of course they're not going to tell you they want your money!

So, let me tell you why this happens and what I've learned about "social media" over the past six years. In the last few chapters, I'll give you the essentials—the basics of every marketing book that actually work. Thanks in no small part to the litany of mistakes I've made (enough to fill a whole other book I want to call *Astonishing Tales of Mediocrity*), I know what *does* work when it comes to marketing. The fact that you're reading this book is proof of that.

And what does, and doesn't work when it comes to marketing? Almost nothing, unless you have a multimillion-dollar budget and a healthy media presence, almost nothing you do outside of the basics is going to help. How did I come to this conclusion? You name the platform, and I can tell you I've used it to promote something, and failed horribly and hilariously at doing so. And if you're reading a book called *Social Media Is Bullshit*, I'm willing to bet you've had similar experiences.

Realizing that little of what's advertised as marketing actually works, I left the marketing profession for good in August 2010. In the six years I spent as a marketing consultant, and given what I learned in the ten years I've been promoting myself and my columns on the Web, I've learned that taking your fee out of the equation is the only way to give someone honest advice that's going to be useful. In an actual consulting role, you get all of the blame, none of the credit, and you can be guaranteed that your client will only listen to half of what you say, and that's only if they like what they hear. Although you don't have to lie to your clients, you have to walk on eggshells with them to make sure they keep paying you. Since I'm no longer a marketer, I don't have that problem.

Most marketers know, even if they won't admit it, that *all* marketing[2] is bullshit beyond . . .

1. Making a good product.
2. Making your product easy to open, easy to understand, easy to use, and easy to share.

3. Making people get behind your product by giving them a story to invest in, by using the traditional media. (That's radio, television, and yes, even the newspaper.)

4. Making adjustments to improve your product based on customer feedback without sacrificing its identity.

Think of your grandmother for a second. Whether or not something is a "good" product is subjective, but if you're able to explain what your product is to her in a way that she understands (to borrow from Einstein[3]), you've got the basics down. Now you know what to say to everyone else when talking about your product. That's all marketing is: making Grandma happy.

What's going to make Grandma happy? I don't know. As it turns out, there is no ideal Grandma.

And that's the rub. People don't want to pay for "I don't know, you figure it out." Lucky for marketing authors, their audiences aren't people to begin with. They're corporations. Some of this is out of necessity. A potential author's book is going to be much, much more attractive to a publisher if she can commit to buying a set number of books as part of their agreement. This puts many marketing authors in the position of having to focus their material on corporations who can commit to buying those books.

For the most part, though, the reason the marketing industry—and that's what it is, an industry—targets corporations is not out of necessity, but greed. Big corporations have deep pockets. So, most marketing advice isn't geared toward helping Grandma appreciate your product. It's geared toward what the research-based advisory firm, the Altimeter Group, describes as an "enterprise-class corporation": businesses with a thousand employees or more.[4]

But what works for an enterprise-class corporation won't work for you. You don't have the investment that people make in large compa-

nies or their products, which comes from year
dollars—spent on marketing and having peop'
those products through media.

To get people to invest in you and your pro
need to reach a critical mass that, in most cases, require
lots of time, a team of people who know what they're doing, mea
sure, and a Don Draper or two. None of which you can acquire on the
Web. This is in part because by nature, it's a niche platform, and in part
because not all things that can be accomplished by large corporations
can be accomplished by you. It shouldn't come as any surprise then that
the top fifty Facebook pages, aside from one generic page for "music,"
all feature celebrities, large corporations, and popular brands.[5] Ditto for
Twitter's top fifty most-followed accounts[6] and the most popular You-
Tube channels.[7] The Top 10 Web Brands, as reported by Nielsen, also
featured a Who's Who of some of the most powerful corporations in
America.[8]

The thing is, marketers can't just come out and say, "I wrote this
book for Pepsi, but buy it anyway because if it sells, I can charge them
more as a speaker and consultant." No one would buy that book. Not
even Pepsi. So, instead, professional marketers try to make their books
appear as if they're going to be useful to you, which is where all that bad
advice comes in. It's hard to fill 230 pages when the basic stuff, the stuff
that actually works, takes up a couple of chapters, at most.

Still, a guy like Malcolm Gladwell, whose books sell ideas that have
no relation to your business whatsoever, routinely makes between eighty
and ninety thousand dollars for his speeches to corporations.[9] So others
follow suit—from marketers like Chris Brogan, to Cyber utopians[10] like
Tim O'Reilly, analysts like the Altimeter Group, selling big ideas of
questionable value to these corporations, that are irrelevant to your
needs.

The book deals, TV appearances, six-figure speaking engagements,

a-priced consulting fees fuel this industry and act as a financial
tive to those looking for a piece of the action. So they coin buzz-
rds, hop onto the nearest bandwagon, and sometimes make shit up to
generate business. Collectively, this is what Harry G. Frankfurt, professor emeritus of philosophy at Princeton University, might describe as
"bullshit."[11]

> When an honest man speaks, he says only what he believes to
> be true; and for the liar, it is correspondingly indispensable that he
> considers his statements to be false. For the bullshitter, however, all
> these bets are off: he is neither on the side of the truth nor on the side
> of the false . . . . He does not care whether the things he says describe
> reality correctly. He just picks them out, or makes them up, to suit
> his purpose.[12]

## CHAPTER FOUR
# SOCIAL MEDIA IS BULLSHIT

**THE GENERAL BITS** of advice I'm going to give you in Part Four of this book have all been said before. In fact, they'll be said again and again until the anti-Christ appears in the form of a six-headed Ryan Reynolds, arguably the worst actor of our time. That is because marketing books are really self-help books for people with money. Those books aren't saying anything new or anything you don't already know. They're just providing the validation people need to get things done. But that doesn't make everything said in those books useful or even true. For example, since 2003, when "The Universal Break-Up Card" went viral, I've been getting e-mails along the lines of the following on a regular basis:

> "In Gary Vaynerchuk's *The Thank You Economy*, he said, 'If you've already experimented with social media and it didn't work, there are only two possible reasons: Your product or service isn't any good, or you're doing it wrong.' I'm doing the rest of the stuff this and the other marketing books tell me, and it's still not working. Am I doing it wrong?"[1][2]

No. You're not doing it wrong. The nongeneral advice, the stuff marketers pad their books and speeches with after they've given you the generic advice and the pat on the back, is simply wrong. I wasted a lot of time and money, mine and others', on social media strategies that I thought worked. It wasn't until the seventh or eighth time that I realized, "You know what? Maybe it isn't me. Maybe it's the tools I'm using. Maybe what these marketers claim simply isn't true."

So, I started to ask around. First, I asked other content creators what they thought. Then I started to talk to people who understand the culture of the Web and how things spread. I talked to the guys whose aggregators used to be the difference between one hundred You-Tube views and a million, and countless others. Within those interviews, my own research, and experience using every Web platform and tool that has rolled out since 1998, I started to reach one inescapable conclusion: Social media is bullshit.

Even those same marketers, who are peddling the myth of social media, agree that it's bullshit. As Joseph Jaffe said to me, "Certainly any marketers that think of any tactic, platform, tool and/or technology as a siloed panacea would probably fall into one of two buckets: very young and/or inexperienced. For the most part, I think the vast majority of tenured marketing would think otherwise. If anything, they're skeptical and/or need education or convincing so as to test, experiment, or invest accordingly."[3] Jeff is right, but you know what the problem here is? Most marketers aren't tenured professionals. They're inexperienced, young, and as I'll show you, simply participating in a gold rush that rewards people for selling bullshit.

And when I pressed Gary Vaynerchuk, who I count as a friend of mine, on his statement from *The Thank You Economy* and what his definition is of "social media" he told me: "It's the Internet." He added, "It's the modern word for it. It's the new word. You know the word that got me into this world was Web 2.0. Remember? You know what social media is? It's Web 2.0. You know what Web 2.0 was? It was the Internet. It is the maturity of the Internet itself." If Gary had said "The Internet" in this passage from *The Thank You Economy*, I'd agree with it but since Gary said "social media," and *many* new and inexperienced marketers take their cues from Gary, the myth of "social media" spreads, even if the guy they're taking their cues from doesn't believe in the myth himself.

This book is a funny, honest take on the myth of social media, the people who fuel that myth, and the only marketing book you will ever need. Here I'll explain why "social media," as we've been led to understand it by marketers, doesn't exist. We'll also consider the players who help perpetuate the myth. We'll take a look at the machinery that makes the bullshit spread, with an examination of what I call The Asshole Based Economy. Finally, we'll look at the basics everyone needs to know about marketing. I've bought hundreds of these books over the years, and found that most of them managed to say absolutely nothing for 230 pages. This book was engineered to be a different kind of marketing book, one that will tell the truth, save you money, and hopefully make you laugh along the way.

So, let's talk about the myth of "social media." Because while it's one thing to declare something to be bullshit and point out the flaws, it's another to suggest that it simply doesn't exist.

# PART I

# SOCIAL MEDIA IS BULLSHIT

---

I am a firm believer in the people. If given the truth,
they can be depended upon to meet any national crisis.
The great point is to bring them the real facts, and beer.
—*Abraham Lincoln, former president and vampire hunter*

# CHAPTER FIVE
# THERE IS NOTHING NEW UNDER THE SUN . . . OR ON THE WEB

**Do you remember Xdrive?** These days it's a footnote in larger stories about MySpace, but in the late 1990s, Xdrive offered people the chance to back up and access their files online.[1] Around the same time, former Oracle CEO and current executive chairman of Google, Eric Schmidt, bet big on the Network Computer (a diskless desktop) that would use the Web as your hard drive.[2] It didn't take. Neither did Xdrive. So, the idea behind putting your stuff online and accessing it from there isn't new. In fact, Western Union was talking about that concept as far back as 1965.[3] The only thing new about the idea is a name: the "Cloud."

Come to think of it, the Web hasn't changed much since the late '90s. Consider:

| 2012 | 1999 |
|------|------|
| Google (Search)? | Google |
| Dropbox? | Xdrive |
| Apple's App Store? | CNET's Download.com[4] |
| Wordpress.com? | GeoCities |

| | |
|---|---|
| Blogs? | LiveJournal |
| Twitter? | AOL Instant Messenger |
| Podcasts? | RealAudio; RealPlayer |
| Ustream? | Lifecasting; Web sites like Pseudo.com |
| Facebook? | SixDegrees; Classmates.com; many others |
| Groupon? | uBid.com; Coupons.com |
| YouTube? | ShareYourWorld.com[5] |
| Wikipedia? | Everything2 (launched as Everything1) |

Are the 2012 services prettier, faster, and easier to use? *Absolutely.* That has a lot to do with the improvements in how they're built and how they're accessed. But they're not fundamentally different from their predecessors. So, if it's true that there's "nothing new under the sun,"[6] or the Web, then why do we keep hearing buzzwords like the "Cloud," which describe these old things in new ways?

Well, there was one pretty huge change to the Web in its twenty-one-year history that often goes unmentioned, and that goes a long way toward explaining what's going on and why everyone is seemingly a "social media" marketer now.

Consider "Vendorville," an article by Pulitzer Prize–winning journalist, Jim Yardley, published in *The New York Times* in March 1998.[7] The gist of "Vendorville" was that Walmart's growth changed the formerly rural and isolated Bentonville, Arkansas, into a place where vendors who want to do business with Walmart congregated. Walmart, whose first store opened in Bentonville as Walton's 5&10, took what was a relatively undeveloped city in the Ozarks and made it their own.[8]

The Web has created its own version of "Vendorville," only instead of Walmart at its center, there are corporations. Big conglomerates with even bigger marketing budgets. And swarming around those corporations, looking for a piece of the pie, are professional and amateur marketers.

Before I go on, let's make this one point clear: The Web—that great democratizer—is essentially run by major corporations.

It's true no matter where you look. Take blogs. These were one of the first, most important places on the Web to make your voice heard.

But where you saw an outlet, corporations saw an opportunity.

These days, of the top fifty most popular blogs on the Web, as ranked by Technorati, the majority are owned by media conglomerates, including Time Warner, Google, Netflix, AOL, Abrams Media (owned by ABC News *Good Morning America* legal analyst, Dan Abrams), Yahoo!, Tribune, and The New York Times Company.[9] Here's how the ownership breaks down for the top ten blogs on the Web according to Technorati:

1. The Huffington Post (owned by AOL)
2. Mashable (a privately held corporation)
3. TechCrunch (owned by AOL)
4. Engadget (owned by AOL)
5. Gawker (owned by Gawker Media)
6. Gizmodo (owned by Gawker Media)
7. ThinkProgress (owned by the Center for American Progress[10])
8. The Daily Beast (owned by The Newsweek/Daily Beast Company)
9. TMZ (owned by Time Warner)
10. Hot Air (owned by Salem Communications)

As technology editor of *Newsweek*, Dan Lyons told me, "I think the golden era of one guy blogging his thoughts and building an audience is kind of over. Some, like Andrew Sullivan, have built staffs and gone in-house at big media companies. Others grew organically, like TechCrunch, but they end up also housed inside a big corporate owner. Most of what I read online are I guess what might still be called 'blogs,' but not really—they've all become mini newspapers now."[11]

And how about Facebook, the most popular destination on the Web for Americans?[12] Facebook has made billions collecting, aggregating, and selling the personal information of their users, and thanks to rampant cloning and customer lock-in, it has become difficult for users to leave and join another service. With the amount of cash and clout Facebook has, their ability to attract top engineers, and their critical mass of users, Facebook possesses a virtual monopoly in the field of social networking, cloning the best features of their competitors to stop them from becoming threats to their market dominance. For example, when they first tried buying Instagram, and were unsuccessful, Facebook added similar photo filters to the ones Instagram provides in their app. The real-time nature of the News Feed and the "Like" button was a knockoff of FriendFeed, a service, like Instagram, Facebook would later purchase. "Places" was a knockoff of foursquare. The "Smart Friends List" was a knockoff of Google+'s Circles. The subscribe feature was a knockoff of Twitter (as were the inclusion of @ replies). Not only is the "Timeline" feature a knockoff of what Time lines.com was enabling users to do, but prior to Timelines.com suing Facebook to protect its trademark, Facebook had allegedly been rerouting traffic from Timelines.com's Facebook page to Facebook's own "Introducing Timelines" page. (A practice Facebook discontinued only after a court hearing.) Even going back to Facebook's origins, Face-Smash, the first Web site Mark Zuckerberg made while at Harvard, was strikingly similar to HotorNot. And yes, even the idea for Facebook might have been ripped off, depending on who you want to believe.[13]

Then, of course, there's the monolithic Google. Google has become synonymous with search, becoming the worldwide leader and holding a nearly 70 percent market share in America.[14] Google's market dominance has changed the search landscape so much so that "google" has become a verb that can be found in the dictionary. I asked Search Engine Land's Danny Sullivan, a respected search industry observer, how much of search engine optimization can be described as "Google Optimization," and he replied "probably 99 percent of it."[15] Google's closest competitor in the search business, Bing, is owned by Microsoft. And Microsoft ain't exactly a mom-and-pop store around the corner. In fact, Microsoft has lost $5.5 billion since they decided to go head-to-head with Google, and $9 billion since they made their search division's financials publicly available in 2007.[16] Unlike with social networking, though, some remain optimistic that they can break through and be successful. Gabriel Weinberg, founder of search company DuckDuckGo, told me, "We believe the search market is opening up in a similar way to the browser market started opening up a few years ago. As such, we believe there is competitive room for a number of search engines that offer different search experiences. We're not setting out right now to be the top search engine, but to offer a different and compelling search experience that some real percentage of people prefer." And he might be right. Unlike Facebook, Gabriel added, "Google doesn't have a history of buying search companies or trying to impede on their growth."[17] The challenge for entrepreneurs like Gabriel, though, is that if Microsoft is losing billions on search by offering an alternative to using Google, how can he and others survive against a billion-dollar corporation with such an entrenched cultural presence? I'm not sure they can.

But in any case, it's an inescapable fact: If you're on the Web, you're lining the wallets of these big corporations through everything you do.[18]

And what does every marketer know best about corporations? That they're wasteful. What happens in most of these companies is that a set amount of money is put aside each year for each department. That money must be spent. *All of it.* That includes marketing, regardless of whether what that division spends its money on actually works.

And in the same way that thirteen hundred vendors have flocked to Bentonville for a piece of the Walmart action, tens of thousands of professional and amateur marketers have been drawn to corporations looking to help them spend their marketing dollars on the Web (and, of course, collect a fee along the way).

Marketing departments aren't going to give marketers their money unless they know what they're spending money on works. But since many don't even know what "social media" is, they've created room for marketers and others to fill that information gap—with bullshit. That's why so many marketers focus on "education" in their books and speeches. Did you ever notice that? Look carefully at the next marketing book you read, or listen carefully to the next speech they give. There's almost always something in there about how some companies "get it" and others don't, and that you have to educate those who don't to understand these "new" metrics. Metrics like "trust," "community," and "engagement." There aren't many MBAs out there who will tell you with a straight face that those metrics make any sense. (And if there are, you should see if they have anything to gain financially from saying so.)

"Social media" is the flavor of the month.[19] But selling bullshit is nothing new, and what kind is being sold changes from year to year. In the late '90s marketers peddled "search engine optimization" (SEO), in the early 2000s "new media," and then "blogging." Since 2007 it's been "social media," in 2011 it was "gamification." Now in 2012 the buzzword is "big data." When "gamification" and "big data" run their courses the marketers will move on to something.

And they'll do so in increasingly obnoxious ways. They must, in order to stand out from the incredible growth of amateur marketers and other "experts" that have appeared since the Great Recession began in late 2007. For example, the day after Amy Winehouse died, The Huffington Post ran a piece titled, "Amy Winehouse's Untimely Death Is a Wake Up Call for Small Business Owners." The person who posted that harrowing warning to small business owners? A marketer, who is "passionate about building brands." Well, maybe not Amy Winehouse's brand . . . but *yours!*[20]

Remember: The people who get rich during the gold rush are rarely the people digging for gold. It's the people selling the shovels. Google Samuel Brannan sometime. You'll see what I mean.[21]

# CHAPTER SIX
# SHOVELS AND SHARECROPPERS

**GEORGE CARLIN IS** a hero of mine. So it shouldn't surprise you that I share his love of words and how they're used and abused by people with power. When talking about poverty in his second book, *Napalm & Silly Putty*,[1] Carlin gave this example as to how we abuse language to hide the truth: "Poor people used to live in slums. Now the 'economically disadvantaged' occupy 'substandard housing' in the 'inner cities.'"[2] In explaining why the language changed, Carlin said, "Smug, greedy, well-fed white people have invented language to conceal their sins. It's as simple as that."[3]

That neatly sums up the message of this book. Is Twitter right for you? Nobody knows. It's impossible to give you advice, and have it be as useful to you as it is someone else. It all comes down to you, your specific set of circumstances, your audience, your timing, and a tremendous amount of luck. Twitter is just a platform. It's not good or bad, useful or useless; however, we've allowed "smug, greedy, well-fed white people" to create a myth around it that says otherwise. A myth that says all you need to do is use the Big Six "social media" platforms

(Facebook, Twitter, foursquare, LinkedIn, YouTube, Tumblr) and all your problems will be solved. All the while, these companies and the marketers pushing the myth are lining their pockets. The marketers by selling you and those companies bullshit, and some of those companies by selling your information to others and monetizing it.

The value of these companies to their shareholders and advertisers comes from the content you make using those services, making them incredibly wealthy, and giving you little beyond the vague promise of "exposure." During paidContent's 2011 conference, Arianna Huffington, head of The Huffington Post Media Group, compared blogging for The Huffington Post to appearing on *The Today Show*.[4] But as an analysis by *The New York Times* FiveThirtyEight political blog showed, the traffic for posts by noncelebrities on The Huffington Post are much like the traffic for most of the stuff uploaded to YouTube: nonexistent.[5][6]

Nicholas Carr, author of *The Shallows*, described this as a sharecropping system in a blog post from December 2006, saying, "By putting the means of production into the hands of the masses but withholding from those same masses any ownership over the product of their work, [Web 2.0] provides an incredibly efficient mechanism to harvest the economic value of the free labor provided by the very many and concentrate it into the hands of the very few."[7] I asked Carr if he thought this situation had grown worse since his post, to which he replied, "I think that, with the rise of social networking in recent years, the sharecropper model has spread and become even more entrenched on the Web. It's the underlying business model for Facebook and Twitter as well as for popular review sites like Yelp and news sites like The Huffington Post."[8][9]

And the depth to which these companies sink to continue generating this content should alarm you. The Huffington Post launched a section that's operated by fifteen- and sixteen-year-olds called "Huffpo High School," where they informed parents, "Although HuffPost bloggers aren't paid, the site offers a widely read platform from which to share their views."[10] *Forbes* contributor Jeff Bercovici, who often documents the activity of The Huffington Post, explained the pitfalls for children contributing to Huffpo High School:

> There are a couple potential problems with using minors to supply the grist for a for-profit enterprise. There's a reason we have strict laws governing child labor. Kids aren't allowed to enter into certain types of work arrangements that adults are because we recognize that they're at greater risk of being exploited. So if you already think Huffpo's model is exploitative—and there are good cases to be made on both sides of that debate—then you're bound to think expanding it to kids makes the exploitation a lot worse. Then there's the whole issue of protecting children from themselves and their own incompletely developed powers of judgment. Just because a kid writes something doesn't mean it's okay to publish it. If a thirteen-year-old writes something overly personal about, say, her parents' divorce, or her sexual awakening, or how she tried marijuana, there has to be someone exercising the judgment to prevent that from being published. If that someone has traffic targets to hit, it increases the possibility that he or she will make the wrong decision. Again, it's an important distinction that we, as a society, make between children and adults. It's perfectly ethical to let an adult writer publish something that will haunt his Google results for the rest of his life; it's not ethical to let a tween do it.[11]

In California, *The Sacramento Bee* reported Facebook "spent more than $102,000 on lobbying in California and made its first contributions to political campaigns in the state. It has taken lawmakers out for lunch in Sacramento, hosted them at its Bay Area headquarters and lobbied on bills concerning Internet privacy, commuter benefits, and use of 'social media' by registered sex offenders."[12][13] These efforts may have contributed to the defeat of a bill in California that would have made "more user information private." In addition to hiring two former FTC commissioners as lobbyists, Timothy Muris and Mozelle Thompson,[14] Facebook also spent more than $1.3 million on its Washington lobbying efforts in 2011, according to OpenSecrets.org.[15] [16]And when they're not defending themselves from charges of flouting FTC rules and regulations concerning the privacy of their users, Facebook is spending money on things like eliminating the Children's Online Privacy Protection Act (COPPA). COPPA prevents children from using Facebook, and Facebook from collecting and aggregating information about them to sell to their advertisers.[17]

Meanwhile, marketers have put six very different platforms under one umbrella, and pretended to give advice that would seemingly work across all of them. But the Big Six (seven if you count Google's search engine as a platform) are very different from one another. Twitter is not Facebook. Facebook is not foursquare. YouTube is not LinkedIn. They have very different audiences and uses.[18] For example, the teenage girls that populate Tumblr would tell you the older business professionals that use LinkedIn are creepy, and they would be right to do so. People who use LinkedIn are fucking creepy.

Since 2007, the sales pitch from marketers has centered around "social media." Not coincidentally, this took off around the same time the economy collapsed. When you think about it "social media" has all the hallmarks of a get-rich-quick scheme, which fits perfectly with the Great Depression–like conditions many Americans have faced since 2007: You don't need to have any specific kind of skill set to use any of the platforms, and there's little risk involved. And like other get-rich-quick schemes, a few people even got rich, which encouraged more people to participate and buy a shovel.

But like a lot of get-rich-quick schemes, it becomes obvious that social media is bullshit once you start to take a close look at it. However, it's worth pointing out that while a lot of us *know* it's bullshit, many of us don't. And so it's important for us who know "social media" is bullshit to step up and keep the others from being taken advantage of.

So, what makes up the myth of "social media," and how can we identify it in order to warn the others?

# CHAPTER SEVEN
## YEAH, THAT'S THE TICKET!

———————

**TO UNDERSTAND THE MYTH OF** "social media" we have to first look at where it came from: Web 2.0.

As I pointed out earlier, creating buzzwords to describe old things in new ways isn't anything new, as is replacing those old buzzwords with fresh ones. In the case of Web 2.0, the term declined around the same time social media started to pick up in usage. And if you look closely at the creation of Web 2.0, you'll see the same stuff that's being played out with "social media." Specifically, that the term's origins may have been pure and well-intended, but because of either an information gap, or the lack of any real need for it, the term's usefulness quickly expired.[1]

First used in publication by Darcy DiNucci, in a piece called "Fragmented Future" for *Print*,[2] Web 2.0 would soon go from a useful shorthand used among developers, designers, and tech companies, to a term that was meaningless to those beyond a certain circle of media professionals, marketers, analysts, and Cyber-utopians. It was then abused by some of those people to better position themselves financially.

Tim O'Reilly, who is often credited with popularizing the term

Web 2.0, told me, "I would distinguish between a lot of the core ideas of Web 2.0 and the name because I've been working those ideas long before the term and continue to work them long after the term. I think the ideas are incredibly useful, otherwise I wouldn't continue to promote them. I think the term was extremely useful and extremely powerful for quite some time. And it continues to have some resonance. Even though people largely misunderstood it."

O'Reilly, much to his credit, does cop to Web 2.0 being a marketing term:

> When Dale Dougherty first came up with it, it was a marketing term. It was a hook for a conference, and that's all it was. And a lot of it was, "How do we reignite enthusiasm in the computer industry? How do we get across that it's not over, after the dot com bust?" And it did exactly what we hoped for. It did reignite enthusiasm. It did get people to go, "Oh my god it's not over." So it was extraordinarily effective at what it was designed for. . . . The core idea, the marketing core idea, you know, "The Web is coming back after the dot com bust," that was the two part. It wasn't like it was [referring to] a new version of the Web.

But it's important to keep in mind that Tim O'Reilly is a businessman. He is the founder of O'Reilly Media, creator and host of the Web 2.0 conference (now the Web 2.0 Summit), investor in services like foursquare, and an author. He took a term that had been floating around since 1999, and built a series of annual conferences around it. The second conference, as Y Combinator cofounder, Paul Graham, pointed out in his essay on Web 2.0, was described by *Wired* as being attended by "throngs of geeks."[3][4] As it turns out, "The conference itself didn't seem very grassroots. It cost $2,800, so the only people who could afford to go were VCs and people from big companies." In other words: enterprise-class corporations. Remember them?

Graham, who wrote what's often cited as the primary essay attempting to define the term Web 2.0, in 2005, discussed the term's rapid obsolesence: "Web 2.0 means using the Web the way it's meant to be used. The 'trends' we're seeing now are simply the inherent nature of the Web emerging from under the broken models that got imposed on it during the Bubble." As Graham acknowledged in his essay, the Web was *built* for creating and sharing.[5] Saying that "Web 2.0" represents something beyond that is misleading and dishonest. But, that's exactly what happened.

Like "social media," as used by people with a financial stake in the myth, there was never a clear definition behind Web 2.0 as a buzzword. Sir Tim Berners-Lee, the man who invented the World Wide Web, told IBM's DeveloperWorks in 2006: "Web 1.0 was all about connecting people. It was an interactive space, and I think Web 2.0 is, of course, a piece of jargon, nobody even knows what it means. If Web 2.0 for you is blogs and wikis, then that is people to people. But that was what the Web was supposed to be all along."[6]

What brought the Web 2.0 buzzword credibility was the media, which often contributes to the validation of these words and myths. As Gawker's Hamilton Nolan told me, "It's primarily laziness. Also [true for] SEO. Also, once you train the public to look for certain catchphrases then they actually do look for them so people keep using them in order to get attention. VICIOUS CYCLE."[7] Drew Curtis, creator of the immensely popular Fark.com, added, "[The] media tries to simplify larger concepts whenever possible, and this predates SEO. I remember when the term *Generation X* was coined, folks who supposedly belonged to it objected to being blindly lumped together. The best argument I remember seeing was 'just because there are a bunch of cats hanging out in a park doesn't mean it's a movement.'"[8]

And even though we don't necessarily trust the organizations generating the news, we do trust their news more than the information we get from many other sources.[9] Because of that, if the media takes a buzzword that means nothing, like Web 2.0, and gives it validation by using it, we'll treat it like it means something, even though we have no idea what that "something" really is.

After the media picked up the term, others started to come around. Even Sir Tim Berners-Lee. In 2009, he told Tim O'Reilly, on stage at the Web 2.0 conference, that he thought Web 2.0 was a "useful term."[10] In 2011, he told me: "Initially, 'Web 2.0' was not very well defined at all, just a buzzword for cool new stuff. As time went on, what had started as mainly the name of the conference became a more defined set of phenomena. This was partly Tim O'Reilly blogging about what it meant for him. It implied things like: user-generated content, interactive AJAX-based client-side apps, and wider reuse of user data for collaborative filtering, etc."[11] But as Tim Bray, developer advocate at Google said to me, "'Web 2.0' is lodged firmly in that period of time; the only usage of the term these days is the lavish, gold-plated, annual 'Web 2.0 summit' put on by Tim O'Reilly and John Battelle. There was no consensus at the time as to what the term meant, it became a marketing vehicle for everyone and anyone. But there's no doubt that that was a time of explosive growth in the Web's feature set and capabilities, and 'Web 2.0' is as good a historical label as any, for use in the rearview mirror."

But was Web 2.0 a good historical label? I grew up with the Web, so I'm a little confused when I hear things about the sudden proliferation of "user-generated content," or the frequent claim that the Web had previously been "read-only," in that you couldn't interact with what you saw in your browser. If it was read-only, what do you call the Web sites and services I mentioned at the start of this section, the ones that provided the same functionality as the ones in use today (though admittedly clunkier)? And how are we defining "user-generated content"? Isn't everything we post to the Web "user-generated"? If we're all publishers, then why do the people who tell us there's no difference between bloggers and journalists tell us there's a difference between what the audience publishes and what the media publishes? There's rarely any consistency with these claims beyond the myth of the week that's being peddled.

I'm not the only who feels this way. As Jimmy Wales, cofounder of Wikipedia, told me, "'User-generated content' suffers in its own way from the same error that 'crowdsourcing' does—rather than being human-centric, it's product-centric. It puts 'content' (which sounds like something that goes in a box) at the center, with 'user-generated' as an identification of which kind of content."[12]

If we're using terms like "user-generated content" to make a distinction between professional and amateur content, why couldn't we just call it amateur content? There's virtually no difference between the two anymore in terms of quality. For every "Friday" on YouTube there's a *Meet the Spartans* in theaters. Sadly, nobody seems to have a good answer for that. The most you get are replies like, "It's a crappy term, but we have nothing else to call it."[13] That's almost as useful as Supreme Court Justice Potter Stewart once saying "I know it when I see it" to describe hardcore pornography. Here's a suggestion: How about we take the platform out of the equation? A movie is still a movie, no matter where you see it or who made it.

## IN THIS UNIVERSE, THE NAZIS WON AND YOUR MOTHER IS A DOG

I always thought there was a disturbing pattern of revising history on the part of those who benefit from the myth of social media and its predecessor, Web 2.0 to benefit themselves.

It's almost as if everything prior to when these guys became "gurus" simply didn't exist. For example, NYU professor Jay Rosen said this about the early days of the Web: "The summer and fall of 1999 is when blogging software first emerged. Prior to that time, Web publishing existed, but you had to know some code to have your own page on the Web. There were people doing a kind of proto-blogging, but they were geeks."[14] I asked Rosen about these comments, and he referred me to a piece *Wired* did concerning GeoCities where they said, "GeoCities continued as primordial version of the everyman's Internet of blogs and Twitter feeds. The personal pages of today are even easier to set up, requiring no knowledge of HTML, and thanks to standard formats, they don't look like ten slot machines trying to burst out of the browser."[15]

However, both *Wired*'s comments and Rosen's comments are inaccurate.[16] GeoCities was, at one point, the third most visited Web site, being purchased by Yahoo! for $3.5 billion in 1999.[17][18] Like LiveJournal, Tripod, and Angelfire, you didn't need to know anything to use GeoCities. They had a WYSIWYG (What You See Is What You Get) editor. You pointed. You clicked. Your Web site went public. As The *LA Times* described it, "At the turn of the century, GeoCities was *nearly ubiquitous* [emphasis added]. Fathers created Web sites about their families; kids created sites about Pokémon; teenage girls created sites about the Backstreet Boys. Practically every facet of culture was documented and thanks to search engines, easily accessible." That doesn't sound like a place packed with just "geeks," does it? Yet here we are, almost fifteen years later, letting Rosen, *Wired*, marketers, and others rewrite history to further their agenda.

Even the use of Wikis, which are considered the centerpiece in most arguments about "user-generated content," Web 2.0, and "social media," began in 1995, a mere four years after the Web was created.[19] I grant that the programming language changed, and that data became more of a focus over time; but that focus on data and the desire for interoperability by programmers and developers is a *cultural change*, not a technological one. The attitude change attributed to Web 2.0 may have been a response to Microsoft reluctantly conceding their monopoly on Internet browsers and desktop software. I'm all for pretending the Blue Screen of Death never existed, but not mentioning the monopoly Microsoft had in the '90s when it came to desktop software and how consumers interacted with the Web is ignorant at best, and misleading at worst.

Napster is another great example of the Web's history being selectively revised. Tim O'Reilly's business partner, Bryce Roberts, described Sean Parker's effect on the music industry as "Katrina-like,"[20] saying "At the time Napster launched, the combined market caps of music labels were roughly $45B. Today that total hovers around $14B and continues to slide. The tools for producing, distributing, and marketing artists, which were once held tightly by only a select few are at the fingertips of even the newest of n00b." (That's cool-guy speak for "newbies.")[21]

*All* of that was Napster's doing? So the post-9/11 recession and the Great Recession that followed, and the consolidation of radio-station ownership mostly into the hands of Clear Channel, and the transition from vinyl to CDs and the fact that CDs were outrageously expensive in the late '90s (which is why the labels had record high profits to begin with), and the loss of MTV and VH1 as primarily music outlets, and the consolidation of major live events venues (also into the hands of Clear Channel, before they spun that division off and merged it with Ticketmaster creating Live Nation), and Apple later taking a cut of the sales, and the dearth of quality acts (the '90s started with Nirvana and ended with Limp Bizkit)—none of those things factored into the decline of those company's market caps?[22] This was all Sean Parker's doing? Really? Wow. That's interesting because Sean Parker didn't even create Napster. Shawn Fanning did. It's not clear what role Sean Parker had at Napster, nor is it clear that Napster had an adverse impact on record sales. There may be some evidence to suggest the opposite is true.[23] The band Dispatch is most often cited in examples of Napster's positive impact on ticket and music sales. As their lead singer, Brad Corrigan, told me, "When Napster was at its peak we had more people interested, discovering, and buying our music than ever before, no question. It was like a dam broke and you could find our music anywhere in the States, regardless [of] whether we had been there before or not. And the large majority of people who liked our music then wanted to buy it." As far as that whole Hurricane Katrina comparison goes . . . well, let's just say Silicon Valley isn't known for its diversity and leave it at that.

This kind of distorted history also finds its ways into stories about the "demise" of print media,[24] suggesting that in a poorly thought-out game of Clue, the killer was the Internet, who did it with the Ethernet cable in the conservatory. For example, venture capitalist Habib Kairouz wrote an op-ed piece for GigaOM (a tech blog ironically funded in part by The New York Times Company through its investment in True Ventures) saying, "The first wave of commercialization on the Internet had a tremendous impact on our lives and has disrupted most—if not all—industry value chains. The print industry was in the eye of the storm, with a decline in readers and advertising budgets forcing many major magazines and newspapers to shut down, while the survivors continue to scramble to deal with the disruption. The primary reasons for the debacle of the print industry were: High fixed-cost structures left incumbents unable to match the niche segmentation requirement and accountability benefits of online advertising. Professional publishers denied consumers' appetite for short form and user-generated content. High debt loads on the legacy businesses created an inability to cannibalize core revenues."[25]

Quick! Guess what's not mentioned? If you guessed . . .

+ The economic recession that followed 9/11 and lasted until the first year of the war in Iraq
+ The Great Recession

+ Corporate consolidation of media outlets that began in the late '80s and picked up in earnest at a time when newspapers had record profits in the '90s

+ Which led to a contraction of positions in order to reduce cost and please shareholders

+ Which also resulted in declining quality of coverage that led to those readers being dissatisfied and going online in the first place

+ Which led to cost cutting in terms of paper, making a lot of newspapers comically small

+ A failure to innovate (also a result of that corporate consolidation and corporate, not local, ownership)

+ Craigslist stealing classified revenues and, to this day, newspapers still not having a worthy response to it

+ An aging readership

+ The people who *did* read newspapers, and whom their advertisers coveted—the rich—migrating to new technology[26]

. . . you would be right. That means you can help yourself to a big pile of nothing! (What, did you think I'd have a prize for you? I'm an author. I can't afford prizes.)

Technology played a role in the decline of the print media, but that's not close to the whole story. And once you get past the gobbledygook of business speak Habib used, we're left with one pretty boldfaced assertion: That there is a consumer appetite for short form and "user-generated" content. That's a very difficult statement to back up. Habib made no effort to do so when pressed in the comments section of that post. Most videos viewed on YouTube, the most popular pages on Facebook, the most popular people on Twitter, and even the top Web brands are *all* from major corporations and celebrities. This is how we spend the majority of our time online, making the amount of time we spend with other stuff like "user-generated content" (or competitors to some of the Web's most dominant brands like DuckDuckGo), very limited. The fact that The Huffington Post, Business Insider, and Mashable, among others came along, squeezed out the choicest bits of other people's stuff (which made clicking-through to the site they borrowed from redundant), and conned advertisers into thinking page views matter doesn't equate to a "desire" for "user-generated content," either. It just demonstrates that, despite their claims to the contrary, that Google's search engine is easily gamed.

There are far bigger societal changes afoot that go beyond the scope of this book. A lot of that stems from technology, like the first wired generation coming of age and airing their grievances using these platforms. But *many* other factors from the Great Recession, the still-lingering residual effects of 9/11, globalization, the "graying" of America, the shift in this country from a manufacturing-based economy to an "ideas"-based economy, and the corporate takeover of America are equally important to consider. None of these factors should be written off in any examination about the use of technology and its impact on the world. Editing them out—as well as the extensive pre-"social media" history of the Web—to further an agenda is wrong, irresponsible, and must be stopped.

# CHAPTER EIGHT
# AND NOW YOU KNOW . . . THE *REST* OF THE STORY

**I**F YOU'RE A MUSICIAN, you might think "awareness" matters or whatever "awareness" actually refers to. You're right. For you it does. But the kind of "awareness" you're looking for may not be available through these "social media" platforms as advertised. If people want to pass your stuff around online, they will, as long as you make it easy for them to do so. But. Your presence on platforms like Facebook and Twitter are redundant. Most of the people who would become fans of yours on Facebook are already going to your concerts, and since the popularity of these platforms lasts as long as Kim Kardashian's marriage did, if you're going to get anything from your fans, it is much more valuable to have it be phone numbers, e-mail, and mailing addresses.

Think of it like this: Except Google, all those services I mentioned in Chapter 5 no longer exist. In ten years, most of the ones you use now won't, either. (Although there's a good chance they'll have the same corporate owners.) But everyone is going to have a have an e-mail address and number they can be reached at. So the claim that you need a presence on these platforms, beyond your own Web site, is bullshit. It's to the marketers' benefit and the benefit of the companies who own those platforms that you use them.

These companies, the marketers, Cyber-utopians, and others spout misinformation. You hear things such as "I found it astonishing that one person can actually have as big of a voice online as what an entire media company can on Twitter" from celebrities like Ashton Kutcher[1], and "The number of people who are your Facebook friends massively dwarfs the number of people who visit your Web site" from Facebook's chief operating officer, Sheryl Sandberg.[2] In theory, the Web and these platforms should allow you to reach a mass audience just by publishing something on it. But it doesn't. The truth is that it's almost impossible for you to reach an audience of any significance using them unless you have a strong network, millions to spend on advertising and publicity, or if the media likes you. Okay, you might get lucky. It's been known to happen. Just ask Justin Bieber.

## HOW YOUTUBE *REALLY* WORKS

Hating on Justin Bieber is easy. But trying to tell people Bieber isn't a "social media" success story is difficult. Any time you look up how Justin Bieber made his big break, you'll see something like this (in this case from The Huffington Post):

> The sixteen-year-old Canadian singer was catapulted from anonymity to superstardom in three years. Living in Stratford, Ontario, at the tender age of thirteen he competed in *Stratford Idol* and posted the videos on YouTube. Ten million views later, he was signed by Usher. Following a breakthrough single, "One

Time," with his debut release of "My World" last November, Bieber had topped 100 million YouTube views.[3]

Let's take a look at the facts: Justin Bieber is talented. (I died a little inside writing that, but it's the truth.) But talent alone can't get you into the majors. People who tell you otherwise almost invariably have something to sell you. The person who wrote this piece for The Huffington Post happens to run a marketing and production company.[4] (Do you sense a pattern forming here?) It's to her advantage to peddle the easy version of the Bieber story because if you buy it, you might buy into her video production and marketing services. So right off the bat, the author driving the narrative of a "social media success story" has something to gain.

But here's the thing: YouTube views are *not* the most accurate way to determine a video's success. Nobody knows how they're calculated except a few people who work at Google, and they're all signed to nondisclosure agreements.[5] (Believe me, I tried to find people who worked at YouTube who would comment on the record about how the views are calculated. Getting someone at Google to answer tough questions is harder than breaking out of a supermax prison in Tucson using only a toothpick and pluck.) What we do know is that there are some algorithms involved because . . . it's Google. Duh. But beyond that it's total guesswork. This is done to keep people from gaming the system, which as The Huffington Post demonstrates, is easy to do, making this policy pointless. People tend to overlook the fact that YouTube is the Web's second-largest search engine, in addition to being one of the most popular Web sites[6], so it's at least understandable that Google would try to keep it from being gamed. Especially because as a video's views grow, it may hit certain triggers to increase that video's exposure. As Felicia Williams, former entertainment content manager at YouTube, told me:

*Whether a video gains popularity organically or through some sort of promotion or feature, there are a few tiers of viewership that once hit tend to expand to more and more views (100k, 1 million, 5 million, 10 million+, 100 million+). If a video breaks any of these benchmarks in the first week, they are 100 times more likely to become a success over time. No one knows exactly how the YouTube algorithms work, but I've noticed that if a video has a big buzz when released and sustains a steady popularity in the first few months, it is somehow marked as very relevant to audiences and is displayed at a heavy rotation as "buzzed about," "popular," or "related video." This relevance ranking increases popularity, which results in more promotion and an exponential growth in viewership.*[7]

If you look closely, you can also see *when* a video took off and *how*, which is a more important part of a video's story on YouTube than how many views it has—especially since videos can get hot if they're uploaded at just the right time, use the right keywords, or hit on something people are searching for. Some of my favorite YouTube performers, The Gregory Brothers, are masters at riding off of hot news and videos, and reaping the benefits. As Evan Gregory told me about two of their biggest hits, "*Timing* [emphasis added] was a huge factor with the 'Bed Intruder Song' and the 'Double Rainbow Song.' When we songify something like a viral video, we're just trying to release from within that video or event, the song that was already there, but was cloaked shyly out of reach of the naked ear. *The sooner we can release that song while the original event is experiencing its own viral moment*, the more the song can amplify the power of that event."[8]

On YouTube, there tend to be three groups, two of which get all the traffic, and a third that makes up the remaining 70 percent of videos—videos that go unviewed. The first group is composed of the mainstream celebrities and companies I've already told you about. The second is YouTube's thriving original creators, many of which have been on the service for a very long time and excel at working with each other, which is partly how they grew their audience. As Evan Gregory told me of their video "Auto-Tune the News #2," "One of the key elements in breaking the video to a wider audience was the fact that it was reposted by BarelyPolitical, a YouTube channel that had (and still has) an enormous following. That exposed their audience to the video, and from there it got shared, blogged about, reported by media and aggregators, etc."[9]

The third group? Suckers like you and I. Almost all of the things we know as viral sensations, or "social media success stories" come from this third group. But there aren't as many as you might think, and trying to recreate their success is nearly impossible. I am not saying that it can't happen. I'm just saying it's incredibly rare and difficult to pull off. There are people out there who are trying to understand the phenomenon but I don't think we'll ever have a clear answer as to why something goes viral organically.

However, very few things spread that way on the Web. They almost always reach a critical mass for very specific reasons, as you'll soon see, and from that we can understand why something actually spreads, instead of the bullshit reasons marketers and their friends might tell you about.

Celebrities have a high-powered megaphone, not to mention a built-in audience. YouTube original creators got in early, built an audience through networking with each other, and got a nice boost when the people at YouTube featured their videos on the service's front page.[10] Given the tremendous impact having been featured by the YouTube staff used to have, it's that much harder now for creators looking to get noticed who don't have that option. The effects of being featured by the YouTube staff aren't something to ignore either. It's made a lot of people wealthy, people who are often cited as case studies in marketing books concerning how you, too, can become a YouTube millionaire. In February 2012, *The Wall Street Journal* ran a graphic featuring the most popular acts on YouTube who were apparently making a lot of money. They were: Ray William Johnson, Nigahiga, Smosh, Machinima, Shane-DawsonTB, FreddieW, College Humor, Fred, RealAnnoyingOrange, and KevJumba. With one exception (RealAnnoyingOrange), everybody else either got on YouTube back in 2006 when YouTube used to feature things on the front page, which in turn blew up the audience numbers for those creators, or already had established and popular Web sites, like CollegeHumor.com. In the case of The Annoying Orange, the filmmaker was already popular on other Web sites such as JibJab.com. *The Wall Street Journal* graphic was championed by folks like Steve Garfield who happens to be the author of . . . you guessed it, a marketing book. One called *Get Seen: Online Video Secrets to Building Your Business*. In the case of YouTube, the entrenched minicelebrities YouTube and Google created by featuring them on the front page seem to be thriving while everyone else is struggling to get noticed.

So when a video from the third group does take off, like Justin Bieber's did, it's important to look into this sort of thing to help defeat these myths.

Almost all videos in the third group sit dormant and unwatched. It's only when someone with clout shares them that they explode. A great example of this would be the "Double Rainbow" video, which was uploaded in early January 2010 and sat unwatched for *seven months* until ABC late-night host, Jimmy Kimmel, tweeted about the video. *After* Kimmel's link went out, and got retweeted by his fans and other notable parties like ESPN's Bill Simmons, the "Double Rainbow" video received 70,000 views. From there, the video took on a life of its own, hitting the activation levels on YouTube that helped it spread further automatically, not to mention placing the video in front of many members of the media who follow both celebrities.[11] If a celebrity is blogging or tweeting about it, you can safely assume you'll see it on a place like The Huffington Post the next day.

When you consider views alone, you're totally ignoring those factors. To say that Justin Bieber was "catapulted to stardom" by YouTube because he has ten million views would be to ignore those facts. If anything, *he* catapulted YouTube to further stardom by fueling the myth that YouTube is a platform you can use to break out on.[12] (This isn't an exaggeration, either; allegedly 3 percent of Twitter's infrastructure is dedicated to serving Bieber's tweets and his follower's retweets.[13]) Don't underestimate the power of this horrible Canadian creature.

To be clear, there are a lot of benefits to using YouTube. As Liz Shannon Miller, coeditor of NewTeeVee pointed out, "Why do people use YouTube? Because not only is it a relatively stable distribution platform, but if you use it right it's a great audience-building tool. Some people are more successful than others. But at this stage there's no better video site to get your stuff out there and also interact with your audience."[14] And she's mostly right. If you're going to use video and host it somewhere, you should use YouTube. However, I disagree with Liz in that you don't need to spend a lot of time on YouTube.com or lose any sleep over your ratings and views. As my brother, Eric, used to say, "If you use it, great, if not, whatever." For what it's worth, YouTube's key demographic is twelve- to seventeen-year-old males, so if you're looking for NPR subscribers, you ain't going to find them.[15] And as I'll show you later, comments and audience interaction on these platforms, while not ineffective, are way overrated.

Also worth noting: How many YouTube views do you think are unique in the first place? In the *Winnebago Man* documentary, attendees of the Found Footage Festival who came out to meet the "The Angriest Man in the World," Jack Rebney, mentioned how often they'd go back and watch the same video whenever they had a bad day or just wanted to laugh.[16] YouTube doesn't break down that kind of viewing for you; you just have to guess.

That guesswork creates an information gap marketers take advantage of. They'll say stuff like: "If you get ten million views, you will get a record deal." But in Justin Bieber's case, someone often gets lost in the "social media success story" narrative: Scooter Braun of So So Def Recordings.

Braun found Bieber on YouTube *by accident*. Braun was looking for someone else and then stumbled across a Bieber video. Braun then approached Justin about representing him. It was Braun who then brought Bieber to Usher. Without Braun, an industry insider, and a healthy dose of luck, Bieber would have never gotten his break. He would have remained at the Triple-A level the rest of his career, sitting just outside of the majors like others on YouTube with high view counts and no record or television deal to show for it.

## SHIT MY FRIENDS LIKE

Some of you might be thinking, "Well, what about Shit My Dad Says? That guy hit the jackpot."

Do people still get lucky and have their stuff spread on the Web or find the right person like Scooter Braun? Absolutely. It's just dumb luck. But for the other 99 percent of us, it ain't happening. That got lost in the narrative of Twitter success story, Shit My Dad Says.

The story, as reported by pretty much every media outlet, was that "unemployed" Justin Halpern started a Twitter feed featuring the very funny stuff that his dad said. The feed went viral, and Justin got a book deal from HarperCollins, which went on to become a mega bestseller, and CBS bought the rights to do a TV show that starred William Shatner.[17] Twitter made Justin Halpern, right? Wrong.

Before the Shit My Dad Says Twitter feed took off, Justin Halpern, reportedly "unemployed," was actually managing editor for Break Media's Holy Taco.com (later a senior editor at Maxim.com). Between Halpern's contacts from working with these properties (which would later cover Shit My Dad Says as it started to blow up), it was easier for him to spread Shit My Dad Says than someone with no network at all. And as you'll hear me say again later: More often than not, people get to where they are today because the people *they* know, know someone who could help them.

Meet Eric Becker, the man behind the hilarious Fake Michael Bay Twitter account, which went viral because of Eric's wit, and to continue the theme of this book, a link from the popular /Film blog. Eric met Justin Halpern through a mutual friend. And as he explained,

> I'm not sure if this was public knowledge, but SMDS was originally Justin's Gchat status at a time when Justin hated Twitter. Justin might still hate Twitter . . . . The Fake Michael Bay following had kept up, and like now, I was occasionally tweeting. I remember having conversations with Justin about how genius I thought the Gchat things were, and I had been pushing Justin to get on twitter for a while. I don't remember if I told him to put the dad quotes on twitter or not, but it doesnt really matter. One day at Social Venture Partners, he sent me the link for the SMDS twitter feed. I think there were seven followers—you know, five woman robots and two friends kind of thing. On the 14th of August 2009, I issued the following tweet with the FMB account: "#followfriday Brilliant: http:// twitter.com/shitmydadsays"; I did another one soon after, and it

*really started to blow up. I remember refreshing the page and seeing
the follower rank just climbing and climbing.*"[18]

Then actor and comedian Rob Corddry tweeted a link to Shit My
Dad Says. And as Halpern told *Time* magazine, "That really made it
viral. [Corddry] jump-started it."[19] When told about the *Time* quote,
Corddry said, "That's nice of him [Halpern] and I do feel an odd kind
of pride. It's an ego boost to be accused of influencing media like that.
But I have to admit that I don't think it's true. Kristen Bell retweeted
him the same day and he was already gathering steam."[20]

Regardless of whether it was Corddry or Bell who made Shit My
Dad Says "go viral," celebrities—real or fake—have the ability of making or breaking products on the Web. And sometimes that effect can
be subtle. Yes, Usher is the name you see most often connected with
making Justin Bieber famous, but Bieber wouldn't have got there if not
for the well-connected record executive who found him. Usher just
gets the credit. Other times it's less subtle, like when demonic hell
spawn Kendall Jenner links to your comedy account and makes it go
viral. For example, it was Kendall who brought Brendan Hampton's
@thenotebook account 40,000 followers in a single day, just be tweeting "I love @thenotebook."[21]

There's something I like to call the "Nickelback Syndrome." Do you
know anyone who actually likes Nickelback? Of course you don't. Nobody does! Yet, Nickelback remains incredibly popular, exactly because
we think everyone else likes them, otherwise why else would they be on
the radio? So, we pretend to like Nickelback to feel accepted. Never underestimate what people will like to be accepted. Remember the Ma-
carena? (Now, if we're being honest, the opposite is also true. A lot of
people just hate Nickelback because they think everyone else hates
them.) Users of community news Web sites like Reddit and every "social
media" platform suffers from Nickelback Syndrome. So if a celebrity, or

more often the media, gets behind something, you can bet you'll find it all over those networks. As Justin Halpern told me, "I think what both [Rob Corddry and actress Kristen Bell] did, especially Rob, was that they got Shit My Dad Says seen by people that aggressively share stuff online. Diggers, Redditors, etc. Because shortly after Rob tweeted it, it made digg.com, back when digg.com was huge. Back then, if something got on [the] digg home page, it would start showing up in in-boxes of people who just occasionally share online content. People like my mom, and friends who didn't work online."[22]

And as with YouTube videos that benefit from being uploaded and tagged at just the right time, Justin added, "Twitter was just starting to blow up right around that time. Ashton Kutcher had his race with CNN.com to get to a million followers. Twitter was the butt of a lot of jokes. It was just kind of everywhere. And no one really knew what the hell it was for yet, or why you'd want to use it. Neither did I. So when I started SMDS, I think the combination of Twitter being the hot thing, my using Twitter for a specific purpose, and my dad just being a funny guy, all sort of came together."[23]

# CHAPTER NINE
# THE ASSHOLE-BASED ECONOMY

**AT THIS POINT** you should notice some trends emerging. Information is being manipulated by many parties to further their financial agenda. Important details get cut out of Bieber's and Halpern's success stories, the history of the Web is being revised, corporations are getting rich off your work and consolidating their market dominance to keep competitors out, and the Web is rewarding big brands and celebrities instead of the rest of us. Even though we were told the Web would level the playing field. This raises an interesting question: How do all these myths travel so well? In order to understand that, we need to take a look at something I call "The Asshole-Based Economy."

In 2005, popular business author Seth Godin released a book called *All Marketers Are Liars*.[1] That was a great title, but Godin retreated from it by saying his book's title was just meant to get your attention. He then went on to say that all marketers are "storytellers," not liars and changed the name of his book. But what do some of the best storytellers do? They lie! Even Godin admitted to that in the original version of the book, before changing the title to *All Marketers Are Storytellers*. After ten years in the field, I can tell you the title of the original was right: All marketers, professional and amateur, are full of crap.

It's one thing to package and sell information. It'd be hypocritical for me to have a problem with that (see the book in your hands, if you have any questions). But. It's a whole other thing to package and sell made-up and potentially harmful information to further your own interests. That's the kind of douchery we want to stop. The Asshole Based Economy consists of marketers, the media, and others packaging and selling that harmful bullshit to further their own interests. By understanding how the Asshole-Based Economy works, I can show you how these myths, like the myth of "social media," spreads.

Chris Brogan is the coauthor of *The New York Times* bestseller *Trust Agents*. For an established marketer like Chris, who has a cult following of smaller marketers and clients soliciting his advice, it's easy to move the required number of hardcover books to get the attention of *The New York Times* "News Surveys" department; the department that determines what gets on *The New York Times Best Seller* list.

How Chris built and keeps that cult following of smaller marketers around is by being an early adopter. Like other marketers today, Chris gets his information from popular "Cyber Hipsters" like former Microsoft employee turned Rackspace employee, Robert Scoble, former MSNBC and Tech TV personality Leo Laporte, former Tech TV personality and Digg cofounder Kevin Rose, former Tech TV personality Chris Pirillo, O'Reilly Media founder Tim O'Reilly, and tech blogs like TechCrunch, CNET, GigaOM, ReadWriteWeb, Gizmodo, and Mashable. If the Cyber Hipsters or the tech media are talking about it, you can bet Brogan and other marketers like him will be talking about how good it is for your business that same day.

## MEET THE CYBER HIPSTERS

I referred to this group earlier as Cyber-utopians because that's the phrase generally used to describe people who love technology and see it as the greatest thing since that time we made up the existence of God. But "Cyber-utopian" doesn't accurately describe the people I'm talking about in this book, nor is it a fair description of some of these parties. Some people just love technology, and there's nothing wrong with that, but most of those people don't have an agenda to push—one that benefits them financially. Cyber Hipsters do.

"Cyber Hipster" refers to two different groups of people who heavily overlap and travel in the same circles. The rhetoric they spew is usually to the effect that people today have the power to do anything without resources, funding, connections, training, education, and so forth. After amassing a large enough audience of willing listeners, they then cash in on the traffic generated from their talk in the form of advertisements, speaking fees, and book deals.

The first group is the early adopter crowd, those that jump on a Web service before the public does and then bitch about how great it was before the public discovered it. As I write this, I'm watching this happen with Path and Pinterest. By the time you read this, they'll start complaining about you using those services. The next time a new service gets announced on a place like TechCrunch, sign up for it and look at who else signed up. Then do it for the next service you reads about. I promise you'll find the same group of people on each of these services, generally being obnoxious and writing posts about how the new service "will change everything!!!"[2] Think of these Cyber Hipsters as the digital equivalent of people wearing trucker hats in Williamsburg, Brooklyn. Nobody likes them, but they want your attention by showing you how cool and savvy they are by being on a service first.

The second group of Cyber Hipsters are those who think the Internet, and by extension the Web, is going to change the world by letting *us* be the media, and that it will also bring everyone else our Americanized version of freedom. That may sound awesome on paper, but it also exhibits a blind arrogance and a disconnection from reality one can only truly experience by living in a bubble like Manhattan or San Francisco. When you hear NYU Professor Clay Shirky refer to Occupy Wall Street[3] or the effort to defeat online piracy bills SOPA and PIPA as "leaderless movements,"[4] he's missing the mark entirely. In Occupy Wall Street's case, the movement was created and operated by Adbuster's Kalle Lasn. Lasn sent mission directives to his Culture Jammers group, who acted as the early occupiers in New York City before the media started to focus on their protests. Later, before the protests were broken up, it was revealed that there had been a small, inner circle of protesters who met separately from the others at Zucotti Park, and were charged with handling the large sums of money the group collected.[5]

In the successful defeat of the SOPA and PIPA bills, what is often left out of "the people's victory" narrative is that none of the previous online efforts of "the people" were successful—or even acknowledged—beyond the Cyber Hipster community, until Google and Wikipedia intervened. They had already been investing heavily in old-fashioned Washington lobbying, and if the bills were eventually put to rest, it was only through their giant publicity stunts: Wikipedia going dark for a day, and Google, one of the top five most trafficked Web sites in the world, directing users to contact their congressmen. As discussed earlier, Google, with assets in the tens of billions and a virtual monopoly on Internet search, hardly qualifies as an arm of "the people."

Cyber Hipsters often argue that the cost of producing content is approaching zero. You can see Chris Anderson arguing this in the book *Free*. That's not really the case for the rest of us,[6] though to some Cyber Hipsters, in their respective industries, it is. And so they just assume that's how it is for everyone else because they live in a bubble. The cost of producing content has gone down, certainly. But there are now other costs you have to factor in that make it just as cumbersome and difficult to get started as it has always been. Think of it like this: Yes, anyone can make a video on the cheap . . . but you need a decent editor to make it look good. That means either *you* have to do the editing (which means taking the time to do so when you can be doing other things) or hire someone to do it for you. And anyone who knows what they're doing won't be cheap either. Especially because there are *way* more "creators" than there are "editors." If you're doing any sort of video editing that also won't be cheap. You should be using a Mac, which means you're going to be out the money of purchasing one of Apple's criminally overpriced computers. Same deal with writing. Anyone *can* write and publish something, and that's a great thing, but in order for it to have a prayer of getting an audience, you need a good editor. That means hiring someone who doesn't think a dangling participle is something that will get you arrested if you take it out on the subway.

## IT REALLY IS A SMALL WORLD (AFTER ALL)

It's no coincidence that a lot of the important Cyber Hipsters that marketers cater to came from established media outlets or corporations before reinventing themselves as Cyber Hipsters. How do you think they got their audience to begin with? Chris Anderson was a journalist for *Wired* before he became a high-priced speaker who talks about business models that don't work in reality. Before becoming a prominent tech blogger, Michael Arrington was a corporate and securities attorney for one of the world's largest law firms, O'Melveny & Myers LLP. And before becoming a marketer and venture capitalist, Guy Kawaski was an early Apple employee, and having anything to do with the inner workings of Apple grants one an automatic fan base of acolytes who will do anything you ask, up to and including murder.

Coming from this kind of background provides some Cyber Hipsters with better access to important parties, and increased attention from the thousands of wannabe Cyber Hipsters out there. That's why you tend to see the same names over and over at those conferences. This has allowed the more popular Cyber Hipsters to better position themselves when fellow marketers, analysts, the media, and corporations are looking for an opinion. Quite a number of popular Cyber Hipsters came from the old Tech TV channel, which was later rebranded as G4 TV. As far as the other popular Cyber Hipsters like Tim O'Reilly go, he's a Harvard graduate. And like in the TV writing business, where Harvard graduates are hired right out of school over other writers solely because they went to Harvard,[7] a lot of Cyber Hipsters can get instant credibility among the tech community with the right kind of diploma. To them, an Ivy League diploma, or a degree from a place like Stanford, who counts founders of such prominent companies as Yahoo!, Hewlett-Packard, Cisco, and Google as alumni, is a signal that you're well connected. Degrees from these institutions open a lot of doors, ones that many of us will never be able to access. Facebook and Zappos, for instance, owe a great deal of their existence to the fact that the key players involved all met at Harvard.

## MARKETERS MAY TELL YOU BOOKS ARE DEAD, BUT THEY NEED THEM MORE THAN YOU THINK

Marketers and Cyber Hipsters working together form a mutually beneficial relationship, spreading each other's bullshit. Cyber Hipsters have their ideas spread to businesses through marketers, increasing their perceived influence, and the marketers get backing from the

Cyber Hipster crowd, which does the same for them. It's important to keep in mind that, according to *Publishers Weekly*, most books don't sell more than five hundred copies. Of those that do, far fewer sell more than the 20,000 or so required to become a *New York Times* bestseller. Twenty thousand books isn't a tough mountain to climb if you have a cult of smaller marketers, businesses, their employees, and fans of the Cyber Hipsters following you around. Having this allows marketers like Chris Brogan to get on that best-seller list quite easily.[8]

The effects of accomplishing this can't be overstated.[9] In 2005, Stanford Business professor Alan Sorensen found that for new authors getting on *The New York Times* Best Seller List, increases book sales by as much as 57 percent. Getting on the list also provides a nice, healthy bump for those looking to cash in with their consulting and speaking fees. So for marketers, the *New York Times* bestseller list is the holy grail.

When marketers lands on *The New York Times* bestseller list, they can leverage their title as a "*New York Times* best-selling author" to mislead others into believing they're an "expert." Without the support of an agent, an institute, a university, or a corporation, the Best Seller list is their best shot at legitimacy—and bumping up how much they can charge potential clients and for speaker fees. Books shouldn't be treated like business cards, but that's what they've become for marketers, Cyber Hipsters, and their friends looking to grow their audience.

Marketers, it bears noting, are also some of the savviest when it comes to gaming Amazon. One publicist I spoke to about promoting this book, who asked to remain anonymous, explained that previous authors he's worked with teamed to promote each other's books, which sent a signal to Amazon's algorithm to suggest their books together when you go to buy one or the other. There have also been other methods employed to game Amazon, including hiring outsourcing firms to create new Amazon accounts and give a client's book a five-star review.

Although they were bound by a nondisclosure agreement not to mention any specific authors, a representative of the outsourcing firm Brickwork India, the outsourcing firm Thomas Friedman and Tim Ferriss have written about, confirmed that they have (and continue to) provide this service for authors.[10]

Which is one good reason why Amazon reviews can be dubious. One study by Dr. Trevor Pinch at Cornell University found that of 166 of the top 1,000 customer reviewers on Amazon, 85 percent of them received free products to review from large corporations.[11] This in turn allowed those reviewers to churn out more reviews and maintain their position (and subsequent power) as Amazon's top reviewers. Similarly, the FTC had to step in when it came to bloggers disclosing when they got free products to prevent people from totally being fooled by the glowing reviews that seemingly follow every time a blogger gets a free product. So clearly the federal government thinks this is a big deal. Richard Cleland, assistant director of the division of advertising practices at the FTC told me:

> *Product reviews are ubiquitous online. There is serious concern whether these reviews are truly independent. Our investigations, for example, [of] Reverb and Legacy Learning have uncovered instances where material connections between advertisers and reviewers should have been, but were not, disclosed. We don't know for sure how extensive this problem is, but based on what we're seeing, it could be quite large. It's fair to say that we are becoming concerned about some aspects of "social media" marketing, depending on how that's defined. Our main concern is the failure to disclose material connections in product reviews. Not just on blogs.[12]*

For marketers, all of this creates a situation where having a book, a printed one, is important, even in an age where the places that hold printed books more and more resemble something out of *Total Recall*. Instead of a Barnes and Noble Online, these marketers are preaching to the converted: People who follow their presence wherever it can be found. And only a small fraction of those can be counted on to buy their book. They have to reach a larger audience to up their speaking fees, and for the foreseeable future, that's going to be a hardcover book released through a traditional publisher, that reaches a bestseller list like *The New York Times*', and not something you can get for $1.99 and a hand job.

## CHAPTER TEN

# THERE'S NO SUCH THING
# AS AN INFLUENCER

---

**IN JUNE 2007,** Brian Solis, author and principal at the Altimeter Group, published *The Social Media Manifesto*. A lot of *The Social Media Manifesto* deals with the concept of influence, declaring, "Monologue has given way to dialogue." But as I've started to lay out for you, we don't influence each other as much as we think we do. The media influences us, and then, stemming from that, we influence each other. This is evident across the Web and can be found on every single platform and in every Web community.

So the following from *The Social Media Manifesto* is not helpful:

> With the injection of social tools into the mix, people now have the ability to impact and influence the decisions of their peers and also other newsmakers. Social media is not a game played from the sidelines. Those who participate will succeed—everyone else will either have to catch up or miss the game altogether. Engage or die.[1]

Yes. It really says, "Engage or die." I'm not really sure how "monologue has given way to dialogue" can be true if one half of that dialogue is telling you that if you don't engage, you'll die. If you figure that one out, you can call me at 518-832-9894.

Let's be honest: Using connections, getting the media behind you, and having a good product are how the world worked before the Internet got here, and that's how it's going to work long after it. The fact that members of the media are obsessed now with what's being said on Twitter, and wrongly treating it as news does not mean people have any more power than they did before "social media" arrived on the scene. Your participation is optional then, not *mandatory*.

I have seen way too many small businesses, artists, and entrepreneurs who think "social media" will allow them to make a career of doing what they love—the exact thing that the marketers have promised them and then went broke in the process. That's why it's important to dispel these myths.

Especially when those myths are so clearly wrong.


## MEETING THE INFLUENCERS IS ALMOST AS USEFUL AS MEETING THE METS


Much "social media" marketing advice is geared toward the idea of finding those enchanted "influencers" and having them spread the word about your product for you. It's a staple of almost every "social media" related publication that's released. I don't dispute that people with actual influence exist, possessing a voice that can reach the seventh layer of Hell from the ninth. What I dispute, and I'm not alone as you're about to see, is that the people who possess this mysterious ability are easily identifiable using services like Klout, and accessed, celebrities notwithstanding. Don't waste your money trying to find, identify, and influence these influencers. If what you do is easy to understand, easy to use, easy to share, and it's good, given enough momentum, it will be passed on. (To a point. More on that later.)

The way many marketing authors tell you to network is wrong. Trading business cards and going to conferences only helps them, not you. They want you to go to these conferences because they get paid to speak at them, and in some cases, they're the ones organizing them, meaning they're making a lot of dough by selling conference sponsorships. (Remember: It's called the marketing *industry*.) That's another reason why their advice is geared toward the enterprise-level crowd. Since managing "social media" comes down to "educating" people about it, corporations often lay out a lot of money for their employees to come see the same old crew of marketers talk about the same old platforms. Mashable.com doesn't expect you to cough up the $499 for a conference ticket; they're charging 499 of your employer's sweet, sweet corporate dollars. And if you think $499 is overpriced, tickets to the 2010 Web 2.0 Summit cost $4,195. In 2011, they adjusted their conference-only ticket pricing to a more "reasonable" $1,545.[2] Wasn't that nice of them?

Although you could make one or two great connections at these things, you're going to make a lot more useless ones. So, go to the conferences and other events if it's something you want to do, not because it'll be an opportunity to "network" or put your product or idea in front of "influencers." Influencers are overrated and almost entirely nonexistent, at least in the way marketers portray them. Are there influential people? Sure. But no one knows who those people are.

The concept of influencers, in the way marketers define them, comes mostly from Malcolm Gladwell's *The Tipping Point*, released in 2000.[3] One of the theories behind *The Tipping Point* was that the difference between success and failure for something is whether a small group of engaged, energetic, and well-connected people get behind it.

Sound familiar? How often have you heard or read about finding the influencers and targeting them in some way to make your product successful? This is what Gladwell called, in his book, *The Law of the Few*.

There are certainly influential people out there. However, with the exception of those mainstream celebrities whose every word is considered news, we have no idea who they are. Could you meet a major influencer at a conference? Sure. But you could also very well meet one at a nightclub on Long Island.[4] And especially at conferences designed to bring in employees from different companies—and to make a profit from those companies—the odds aren't looking much better. No offense to my friends working for The Man, but if they had that kind of "influencing" clout, they probably wouldn't be working for The Man in the first place. It's not that the people going to these conferences aren't important; but any power they may possess to make or break you is probably exaggerated.

And it's not just "social media" conferences. The conference crowd generally consists of fans, employees, curious onlookers, and people looking to make a buck (whether they be vendors, sponsors, or even the conference organizers). How much power they posses is again, and mostly, greatly exaggerated. Proof can be found by talking to any Hollywood insider who has seen the launch of a comic book or graphic novel–based movie at the San Diego Comic-Con, a supposed hot bed of "influencers"—and then saw that movie flop. The awesome *Scott Pilgrim vs. the World* and the less awesome *Watchmen* films are great examples.[5] (This is also known as the *Snakes on a Plane* Phenomenon, where a movie, television show, or other product was incredibly hyped all over the Internet and then failed miserably at the box office or in other offline arenas.) As Tucker Max told me about the commercial failure of his otherwise decent movie, "People don't automatically transfer fandom. Meaning, loving a book and loving a movie are different things."[6]

If the primary user-base of most platforms on the Web (men, 18–49) can't move the needle in a significant way when it comes to translating online buzz into offline results, that should serve as a pretty serious red flag for you about the power of the Internet at large to fuel the success of something without the media or a celebrity's involvement.

## ALL THE WORLD ISN'T ATWITTER

Marketers and others like to claim Twitter took off thanks to the South by Southwest Interactive festival in 2007. This was based on the number of tweets that appeared in response to the conference, which is a bit like using a ruler to measure how long that same ruler is.

Twitter.com's overall traffic, at the time it was proclaimed to be a break out success at SXSXi 2007, was never mentioned. Instead you heard stuff like, "One-line one-to-many messaging service Twitter is aflame during the South by Southwest Interactive conference" on Gawker, which was followed by, "Twitter staffers Jack and Alex tell me that the site, which normally carries around twenty thousand messages a day, broke sixty thousand a day this weekend."[7] And then there was this, from CNET: "According to Laughing Squid blogger Scott Beale, Twitter is 'absolutely ruling' SXSWi. Social software researcher Danah Boyd said Twitter is 'owning' the festival."[8] And this was before third-party clients like TweetDeck, where Twitter's "power users" now do the bulk of their tweeting, came about. So traffic is key here in determining when Twitter actually "took off."

In that regard, Twitter didn't take off until two year later when, Nielsen reported, Twitter.com's American traffic went from 475,000 unique visitors to almost seven million in the months between February 2008 and February 2009.[9] The tweets may have increased during the 2007 SXSW festival, particularly among the Cyber Hipsters, but did the service "take off" in the sense that it became a mainstream thing? No.

Even today it's debatable how popular Twitter actually is. If Pew's research is accurate, only 13 percent of all Americans in 2011 were using Twitter.[10] That's 3,900,000 Americans. Twitter says half of their users log in once a day, and that 40 percent of those "listen" but don't actually tweet anything. So, as that number appears smaller and smaller, you have to wonder, how mainstream is it really? Just because people know what Twitter is thanks to the media hype[11] doesn't actually mean they use it. I know Axe Body Spray makes women want to molest me, but that doesn't mean I buy it.

Consider one popular example: The Twitter's public relations feed, @TwitterComms, reported that Twitter set a "Tweets Per Second" record of 8,868 at 10:35 P.M. Eastern Standard Time on August 28, 2011, the day the 2011 MTV VMAs aired.[12] The time 10:35 P.M. coincides with the moment Beyonce revealed she was pregnant during the show, which was the highest-rated VMAs to air at the time of this writing.[13] (This record would later be broken during the 2012 Super Bowl. More on that in a second.)

On September 1, 2011, Gary Vaynerchuk recorded a video saying, "Social Media is helping drive television ratings up the roof to all-time highs." He added, "The virtual water cooler is happening in real time."[14]

This, upon hearing, almost gave me an aneurysm.

As it turns out, the difference in total viewership between the 2010 VMAs and the 2011 VMAs was exactly one million people.[15] If there are about 4 million Americans on Twitter, and only about half of that number logs in once a day, then it's looking like a stretch that "social media" drove the ratings increase. Some other, more likely, possibilities: The VMAs have been in a ratings upswing since 2007. And the show tends to do well during times of national distress[16] (they had their highest run of ratings between 9/11 and through the first year of the war in Iraq). (And just like the VMAs, the Super Bowl has also been in a ratings upswing since the economy bottomed out.)

So I'm not sold that social media, and specifically Twitter, did much of anything. Most likely, Twitter and other platforms served as a look into what people were already watching. The fact that ratings were also down for such major events as the 2012 Golden Globes and The State of the Union Address, despite a high volume of tweets during the airing of each, only supports this notion.

Unfortunately, a little thing called math didn't stop the marketers, Cyber Hipsters, and tech companies from jumping on the "Twitter = Ratings" and "Twitter = Influence" bandwagon. In the technology blog Venturebeat, Twitter CEO Dick Costolo argued that the 2012 presidential election would be the "Twitter Election," and that "candidates that don't participate on Twitter while the conversation is happening will be left behind."[17] If that were true, it would be guys like GOP candidate Buddy Roemer, who actively tweeted and interacted with his audience during the nominating process, that led the pack, while Mitt Romney, who barely tweeted, lagged behind in obscurity.

And as Governor Roemer told me, despite articles with titles like "How the Internet Saved Buddy Roemer's Candidacy," which ran on Mashable.com, he was not entirely pleased with the results of some of his "social media" efforts, and stated that while Twitter has good promise, "I would not have chosen Twitter if left to my own devices."[18] Roemer told me he was only using "social media" because the actual media didn't allow him to participate in the numerous Republican debates that were held.

## WHO'S YOUR DADDY, AND WHO DOES HE KNOW?

Dr. Duncan Watts, a network-theory scientist and Yahoo! researcher, is most often cited in counterarguments concerning the overvaluation of "influencers." In 2003, Watts recreated the experiment Malcom Gladwell's book heavily relied on, "The Six Degrees of Separation" study by social psychologist Stanley Milgram.[19]

Dr. Milgram was studying the interconnectedness of people. His experiments asked people in Wichita, Boston, and Omaha to attempt to convey a letter to a stranger in a different city. To do so, they were asked to mail it to someone they know on a first-name basis. That person would then do the same, to a recipient who would do the same, until it arrived at its destination. Milgram concluded, in part, that some people are better connected, and therefore much better than others at passing on messages. Gladwell's "influencers."

In Dr. Watt's recreation of the Six Degrees experiment, he found that, in spreading a message electronically, very few of the 61,000 participants in the study sent their message through one of those influencers.[20] This suggests, at least to me, that the influence of the "influencers," as defined by marketers, is negligible.

But it didn't take an electronic recreation by Dr. Watts to see how flawed the Six Degrees study was. In looking through Milgram's notes on the experiment, University of Alaska-Fairbanks professor Judith Kleinfeld found something disturbing.

She told me, "Stanley Milgram and others repeating his work don't acknowledge the obvious fact that most of the letter chains do not get through. He has not shown that people are connected to each other by six degrees of freedom. Moreover, minorities and low-income groups have much lower chances of getting their letters through as people who are Caucasian or well-off."[21]

The myth of "influencers" isn't a new one either. It has been around for half a century. But since *The Tipping Point* came out, marketers have increasingly adopted it into their strategies despite the fact that it was that easy to target a group of influential people and see results . . . well, I'll let Dr. Watts get the last word on this one:

> It's true that there is a striking difference between our ability to identify influential-seeming people after the fact, and our ability to identify and co-opt them to our purposes in advance. Yet of course, it's the latter that is important in marketing (and in most other domains). If the stories we tell about influencers don't help us to predict who they will be in the future, then they're really just stories. None of this is to say that influence isn't real, or that some people aren't more influential than others (although who they are may depend a lot on the specific domain and context)—just that no one (so far) has been able to exploit this observation systematically. I also think that if and when we do learn to identify influencers, we will discover that their influence is less spectacular than certain pop-sociology theories have led us to believe. That doesn't mean it isn't a useful thing to try to do, but anyone hoping to trigger the next social epidemic by targeting the key influencers is probably dreaming.[22]

So, go to conferences and try to find influencers. By all means. But here's a novel idea: Go because you want to, and not because you feel obligated to. You will be in a better place to forge real, valuable relationships if you do, and those are what drive business.

And to be clear: Many people in the social media industry who are peddling the modern version of the "influencer" myth believe themselves to be influencers. Otherwise they wouldn't be talking about useless things like their Klout scores.

Hey, maybe you'll get lucky and meet that one person who can make all the difference. But remember that the majority of people attending are there for the same reason, so you might have some competition.

Think of the TED conference, which costs attendees $6,000 to attend. You go to that sort of thing to meet all the luminaries who regularly appear at TED, but as one attendee pointed out on Tech-Crunch,

> Long story short, from the opening night gala, TED rapidly segre-gates itself into two distinct groups: Group A (the people everyone would love to meet), and Group B (the people who want to meet those people). The people in Group B spend the entire TED conference run-ning around with business cards, hoping for, you know, five seconds of face time with Sergey Brin, Bill Gates, Steve Wozniak, Cameron Diaz, or the like. The people in Group A, on the other hand, spend most of TED trying to avoid the people in Group B. Put the people in Group A and Group B together in a room (the "opening night" gala is the only time this really happens), and the tension is sometimes pal-pable.[23]

So where can you network with better results? Of the "Big Six," only one of them is built to interact with strangers in a meaningful way: Twitter. LinkedIn is a close second, but that tends to work better if you already work in a professional setting. LinkedIn is also pretty self-limiting, too. Someone has to introduce you to someone else. On Twitter, you can follow whomever you want.

And although you could make some good connections online— and I can certainly vouch for that—I've found *offline* connections to be the most meaningful, beneficial, and long-lasting. Online connections are a lot like the ones you make in elementary school. Everything's cool until you pull down your pants during the anatomy lesson.

Instead of starting with the conferences, or the strange and interesting people the Internet has to offer, try starting locally. Start with your friends, then their friends, then people that they know, and keep going from there. You'll find in doing this that you'll almost always hit a connection that not only will be useful, but it'll be someone more reliable and trustworthy than someone you meet online, precisely because it came from a personal referral. (You might also make a friend out of it, something more valuable than a "contact," fan, or follower ever will be.)

# CHAPTER ELEVEN
## ANALYZE THIS

---

**I DON'T SPEND** a lot of time talking about analysts in this book, but now that I've introduced you to Brian Solis, I thought this was worth mentioning. Analysts like Solis and the Altimeter Group make up an important part of the daisy chain in spreading myths about things like "social media." Usually, they represent the third link in the Asshole-Based Economy's line of progression, which looks something like this:

1. Cyber Hipsters
2. Tech Media and marketers
3. Analysts
4. Corporations
5. Mainstream media
6. Us
7. Mainstream media again

The important thing to know about the analysts is that they repackage and reword what they've read on popular tech blogs and then sell that information at a marked-up value to their corporate clients. Forrester Research, for example, will release a paper like, "Case Study: USA Network Wins Over Fans Through Gamification" and then sell that case study to their clients for $499.[1] And when analysts are not doing that, they're releasing questionable information freely in an effort to drum up business for themselves. The most prominent among the social media marketing crowd is the Altimeter Group, whom you've heard me mention a number of times in this book.

The Altimeter Group was founded by former vice president and principal analyst at Forrester Research, Charlene Li. It also has former senior analyst at Forrester, Jeremiah Owyang as a partner. Just as I was wrapping up this book, Altimeter released a report called "Social Business Readiness: How Advanced Companies Prepare Internally."[2] The subheading was, "Social media crises are on the rise, yet many can be avoided through preparation."[3] I'm going to walk you through this report to demonstrate the kind of bullshit you can expect to encounter when reading the work of most analysts.

How to address a "social media crisis" is PR 101: respond quickly but not hastily, be honest, be transparent, apologize, tell people how you're going to address the problem, and then do it. By calling this a "social media" crisis, Altimeter is trying to draw a distinction, and with it, the implication that how to manage a "social media crisis" is different from managing bad publicity. Here, the Altimeter Group said "social media crises" are "on the rise" and then linked to a post put together by Owyang that proceeded to list fifty-three "social media crises" over the past ten years.[4] All fifty-three involving major corporations, and only eight percent of those "social media crises" resulted "in a loss of revenue." The rate of occurrence (using Altimeter's definitions and examples) was ten in 2008, nine in 2009, ten in 2010, and six in 2011. The only sharp increase came from 5 instances occurring in 2007 to the 10 in 2008.[5] Not coincidentally, the same year the economy collapsed and "social media" came to prominence as a buzzword.

In the primary case where a company lost money because of a "social media crisis," it had nothing to do with "social media" at all. French content company Hi-media, who was used in one of those cases by Altimeter, was fined $33,670 by a French court for deleting an entry on Wikipedia that mentioned their competitor.[6] That's not a "social media" crisis, that's just exploiting a well-known issue with Wikipedia, and as I mentioned earlier, Wikipedia (and Wikis) aren't anything new, they are almost as old as the Mighty Morphin' Power Rangers. Messing with your competitor is a good old-fashioned dick move, not a "social media crisis."

The other two examples Altimeter provided where companies lost money both involved widespread coverage by the traditional media. The first was when a CNN iReporter ran a story saying Steve Jobs had died back in October 2008.[7] He hadn't, but Apple's stock price took a very brief hit of 10 percent before recovering 7 percent of what it lost by the end of the day.[8] (Remember the sharecropper model Nick Carr wrote about? That best describes CNN's iReport platform. It allows anyone, whom CNN refers to as iReporters, to upload their own stories, images, and videos—entirely to the benefit of CNN.)

CNN doesn't actually look at what goes on with iReport. It's kind of a free-for-all. That's not a "social media crisis" so much as CNN being understaffed and overwhelmed when it comes to monitoring who is producing content on their Web site. (In fact, just as this book was about to go into production, CNN announced plans to lay off more reporters and increase their focus on content generated by their iReporters. Upon hearing this, comedian Stephen Colbert commented on *The Colbert Report*, "Bold move, CNN, for getting rid of all those pesky professionals. Hopefully this bold move will help you get rid of your remaining viewers.")[9]

But the issue here is not about iReporters being allowed to publish anything; it's about the lack of oversight from CNN and other media companies that have similar platforms such as Forbes, Fast Company, and The Huffington Post, which can cause real harm to people and companies. However, a corporation being wasteful, negligent, and inefficient, that's not a "social media crisis."

In the other case Altimeter provides where a company lost money due to a "social media crisis," GoDaddy's Bob Parsons killed an elephant, and then tweeted about it, which caused people to lose their minds. Special interest groups like PETA picked up the story which was soon followed by national outlets like ABC's *Good Morning America* following suit.[10]

The fact that TMZ also got involved should tell you everything you need to know about this specific story. Forget what Parsons did for a second. TMZ is owned by Time Warner, and so if one news division covers something, especially one as popular as TMZ, you can make a pretty safe bet that their other divisions will pick up the story as well[11] because media executives foolishly believe that what's popular on the Internet in terms of page views will translate into what's popular on television with ratings, despite there being little to any evidence to support this belief. The fact that Parsons posted the pictures and videos of his wacky African adventure on Twitter, which Altimeter claims made it a "social media crisis," is irrelevant. *The platform the incident originated on doesn't matter*, especially when how to manage this sort of thing remains the same.

In response to the temporary media firestorm, Namecheap, a GoDaddy rival, offered GoDaddy customers who were offended by Parsons' behavior an opportunity to switch providers, offering some of the revenue from that switch to Save the Elephants. Save the Elephants received $20,000 after just over 20,000 people left Go-Daddy for Namecheap. This was a revenue loss, but it wasn't a "social media crisis." It was a dumb move on Parsons' part that resulted in bad publicity. (Later, when GoDaddy faced another alleged "social media crisis," this time with a Reddit-led boycott of the service because they supported the SOPA legislation, the effects of the boycott were negligible. Although they lost registrations that day, they made way more than was lost. Due to the media coverage of the protest though, GoDaddy later reversed their position on the SOPA legislation.)

The rest of the "social media crises" aren't necessarily crises either. They're just a new way to describe good old-fashioned bad publicity that's generated from good old-fashioned customers complaining, that's been repackaged and renamed. People getting upset, and then the media picking up that they're upset and calling it news, is nothing new. That's pretty much been the MO of the modern media, especially since Congress passed the Telecommunications Act of 1996, which accelerated the consolidation of the American media into less than a handful of providers. That consolidation brought about a race to the bottom in an effort to attract eyeballs to please shareholders and advertisers. Since that time, if a vocal minority of people are making noise about something, it inevitably becomes a news item. Where they made that noise doesn't matter.

Think of it like this: The people who put the emphasis on the platforms, like the Altimeter Group ("Social Media Crises Are on the Rise"), Gary Vaynerchuk (there's either something wrong with your product, or you're using social media wrong if it's not working for you), and Brian Solis (engage or die), *always* have something to sell you. It's important for them to try to redefine old things like handling a PR disaster, and put the focus on the platforms so it creates curiosity and interest. If they don't, they wouldn't be in business. So the rebranding of PR disasters may be good marketing for them, but it's also bullshit for you.

But, if it's bullshit . . . why are people buying it?

# PART II
# MEET THE PEOPLE BEHIND THE BULLSHIT

---

Nobody ever went broke underestimating
the intelligence of the American public.
—H. L. Mencken, *journalist and satirist*

## CHAPTER TWELVE

# MAYBE "SOCIAL MEDIA" DOESN'T WORK SO WELL FOR CORPORATIONS, EITHER?

IN ECONOMICS, THEY HAVE A term to describe the study of the phenomenon where "experts" take advantage of people who don't know any better, using leverage (like "*New York Times* bestselling author") because there's a financial incentive to do so. It's called *information asymmetry*. In *Freakonomics*, by Dr. Steven Levitt, professor of economics at the University of Chicago, and Stephen Dubner, a journalist and award-winning author, this idea is spelled out nicely: "If you were to assume that many experts use their information to your detriment, you'd be right."[1] Here's an example of information asymmetry with "social media," or as I've dubbed it, the Asshole Based Economy:

On July 20, 2011, *New York Times* bestselling author Chris Brogan offered a two-hour live Webinar called, "Learn Google+ for Business and Networking."[2] He posted a video to entice people to pay for his Webinar. In it he talks about how he's "nuts for Google+," talks about how Google+ has become the top traffic referrer for his Web site, and how it's "early days and time to get in now."[3] The Webinar, for $47, offered an hour of training and an hour of Q & A, teaching people and businesses about:

- Profile tips and tricks.
- Organizing people in circles.
- Finding the good stuff.
- How to post engaging material.
- Keeping up with comments.
- Making the most of your time.

Looking over the offer, it's clear there were a lot of problems with it from the start. (And if we were to add hindsight into the equation, you can see that use of Google+, once it opened to the public, mostly flat-lined.)[4] For one thing, Google+ at the time of Brogan's seminar was around twenty-four days old and was not open to the general public. You needed an invite in order to use the service. So its value for business and networking was a bit dubious at that point. Chris Brogan then claimed to have spent 250 hours on Google+ since it launched. That works out to about eleven hours a day for twenty-four days, provided Chris got his Google+ account on Day One. Brogan, by his own admission in a blog post on July 19, called "A Day in the Life," runs a business, does consulting, updates his blog, tweets, writes columns for other outlets, updates his newsletter, tweets some more, plays with his kids, and, I think it's safe to assume, goes to the bathroom.[5] Given all that, do you think he really spent eleven hours a day tooling around on Google+?

This is a relatively minor point, but it establishes that Chris was exaggerating to get business professionals to pay $47 for his Webinar on a service many of them didn't yet have access too (or even need).

Chris then followed up this claim by saying he was the guy who "made Twitter a business staple in 2006."[6] Twitter wasn't a business staple in 2006. Chris may have joined the service in October of that year,[7] but the general public, and most businesses, didn't join the service en masse until 2008 when the media and the celebrities "discovered" it, as I laid out for you in a previous chapter.

So Chris was batting 0-2 already before he told businesses they had to "get in early" with Google+. But strike three came quickly when Google asked businesses to *stay away* from Google+ at the time of his Webinar. Chris used the example of Ford and their presence on Google+ to justify his claim that businesses should get in early, but Ford's account (like many other business accounts on the service) was deleted the day of his Webinar.[8] Luckily for Chris, Ford's account, unlike the others, would later be restored to much controversy. (It probably didn't hurt Ford's cause that they have been working with Google to use Google's creepy Prediction API to optimize their vehicles, and that they made a joint announcement about it earlier that summer.[9])

Using big companies like Ford is a tactic that everyone backing the myth of social media employs, despite evidence showing that not only does what work for the large corporations not work for you, but there are many instances where this *doesn't even work for them*, either. I'll tell you about those later. Despite this, every year marketers trot out a big corporate "social media success story," saying how it's proof that "social media" can work for you, and every year it turns out that what they present to the public isn't quite the whole story. The problem with comparing a big brand and what they do to what you might do is that they have money, connections, and other resources at their disposal that they can tap into. In fact, a lot of them simply aren't looking at "social media" as a revenue generator, but a loss leader. Running a "social media" campaign may be a financial hit giant corporations can take, but it'd be a pretty significant financial hit that the rest of us can't survive.

Remember: people get pretty heavily invested into big brands, companies, and celebrities that they're exposed to through mass media. So when any of them pop up on these Internet platforms, it's not a shock to get some fans to get behind whatever they're doing. The tricky thing is figuring out whether these fans are new fans or if they are already customers who buy that brand's products anyway. And if they *are* new fans, how many of the brand's fans and followers do they represent?

In August 1997, Web usability expert Jakob Nielsen wrote, "One of the latest buzzwords to agitate the Web is 'community.' In fact, most Web sites have less sense of community than a New York City subway car."[10] Did I forget to mention he said that in *1997*? Quick, google "It's not about you, it's about the community." That's some scary shit you just saw, huh? I wasn't kidding earlier when I said "there's nothing new under the sun," especially when we're talking about the Internet and marketing.

Nielsen also helped apply to the Web the notion of "Participation Inequality" that Will Hill of AT&T Laboratories had originally developed. This term describes how 90 percent of all Web users are lurkers, 9 percent *might* contribute *occasionally* and 1 percent will do the most commenting and participating. This has also been referred to as the 1 Percent Rule, and it has been well documented and observed numerous times over the years. When it comes to all these platforms, you need to be aware of the 1 Percent Rule. Anyone who tries to tell you the number of retweets, views, likes, or blog comments you have matters? Tell them about the 1 Percent Rule. Even the pros could use a gentle reminder. I'm a big fan of Lizz Winstead, cocreator of *The Daily Show*. When I asked her about the Web's impact on how she crafts her stand-up set, she told me, "Well, since I am a topical comic I am responding all day. Twitter is an all day, every day open mike with the world. Twenty-five RT's and it goes into the act."[11] That might work for Lizz because she's been at this long enough to know what's funny, but if you were to ask any comic how their popular tweets do on stage, you're going to find the answer usually is "not well." That's the 1 Percent Rule in action. (You can also see this reflected with TV shows. If the Internet was an accurate measure, NBC's *Community* would be a ratings monster, but it's not.)

So is that 1 percent statistically significant for these businesses? Is what they're going to bring in with revenue going to justify what it costs to obtain that minority of users? There's no easy answer, and it's going to be different for everyone. But saying, if Ford is doing something, so should you, is flat-out wrong and manipulative. If Ford is doing it, you shouldn't. Why? Because in order for something to be approved at a big company like Ford, it's gotta go through many layers of management, not to mention pass approval by their advertising agency, Team Detroit, and a legal team or two. Big companies and big advertising agencies rarely take risks, so if you see a company getting in on the latest thing, you're probably too late to see any benefit from doing it yourself. Think of big corporations as the guy you sometimes run into at parties who's just now listening to Wham! and wearing a Members Only jacket.

The unfortunate thing is that since "social media" emerged as a replacement buzzword for Web 2.0, we've been given four new, big corporate examples of social media success each year, which professional *and* amateur marketers then proceed to parrot in each other's books, speeches, and in meetings with their clients.

So, let's take a closer look at these "successes."

## 2007: BLENDTEC'S "WILL IT BLEND?"

In 2007, the marketers and the media started to talk about what they claimed to be the first corporate social media success story: Blendtec's "Will It Blend?" campaign. First appearing on YouTube in November 2006, the idea came from Blendtec's former marketing director George Wright. As Nate Hirst, global marketing director of Blendtec describes it, "He walked into our demo room and saw wood chips strewn all over the floor. He came to find out that this is how Tom Dickson, owner and CEO of Blendtec, had been testing his blenders since the 1990s. George put together a proposal for the first five blends and asked for a budget . . . Tom gave him fifty dollars. Fifty dollars is what led us to YouTube, we couldn't afford anything else at the time."[12]

In September 2007, Mashable reported on the entertaining videos: "Here's another success story for viral video marketing online. The Blendtec guys have increased their sales five times over thanks to a little segment called 'Will it Blend?'" They then added, "These video marketing ploys are starting to look a lot like the Charles Dickens work-hard-and-save stories that reeked of happy endings in the shifting world of impending industrialization. We've got a new shift going on now, into the digital world, and it's stories like Blendtec's that make us think that we can all be the next LG15 [Lonely Girl 15] or Chris Crocker [The "Leave Britney Alone" guy] (eww)."[13]

That may sound nice on paper, but in practice the reality isn't so pleasant. What's not mentioned is that most videos don't spread organically. Probably less than 1 percent of them do. The rest spread for very specific reasons.

In the case of Chris Crocker, of "Leave Britney Alone" fame, aggregators like GorillaMask, Digg, Reddit, College Humor, Fark, and many others linked to his video, which caused it to spread among other aggregators and then to the blogs.[14] The blogs in turn posted about it until it spread to the larger media outlets. This activated those triggers on YouTube that raise a video's exposure as it hits different viewing benchmarks. So, like the Crocker video, the "Will It Blend?" videos didn't go viral in an organic sense, which is implied in the Mashable post. It spread like the Crocker video because it helped fulfill the business interests of Web sites *like* Mashable, who need to post constantly to trick Google into ranking them highly in search results. Back when the community news Web site Digg had the kind of juice to be the difference between an item spreading to more mainstream users and being left floating in history's toilet bowl, the "Will It Blend?" video featuring an iPhone was a huge hit. And from Digg, the video spread to those aggregators, Web sites, blogs, and mainstream outlets because they all relied on Digg for content the way they do now for Reddit. And if one of them posts a "viral video" you can bet they all will help grab some of that traffic.

More important, "Will It Blend?" launched back when YouTube staff members used to hand-select videos to feature on the front page, which generated a huge bump in exposure for those videos. As Felicia Williams, commenting as an industry observer and *not* as the former entertainment content manager, described it:

> [In 2006–08] the YouTube homepage was just a list of 10–12 "featured" videos that were selected by YouTube's community and content team. Two to three videos were featured a day, each getting an average of one half to three million video views in that three-day time-span. When YouTube moved away from curation, they changed the word "feature" to mean a video promoted by their algorithm. Features boosted not only views but also subscribers. Prior to the home page suggesting videos users will like based roughly on past viewership and participation in the site, there were fewer ways to discover videos. The lack of targeting created a greater reliance on features, subs [subscriptions to a video's YouTube channel], browse, and search to find something worth watching. Since home-page features often resulted in a significant boost in subscribers (who wanted to be able to find the video or channel again later) the feature had a lasting effect on overall channel viewership. Creators who released similar videos of the same quality as the one featured now had a much wider audience for every new video they put out.[15]

Many of the "YouTube Celebrities" you've heard of owe much of their success to this bump, including Lonely Girl 15. A source involved with the production of Lonely Girl 15 videos mentioned to me how big of an impact the series being featured on YouTube's front page had, which then promptly led to stories about the show in *The LA Times*, *The New York Times*, and *Wired*. (*Wired* would later go on to report, again, inaccurately, that Lonely Girl 15 grew in popularity in part due to the involvement of Hollywood talent agency CAA. Although there was someone involved with the production who worked at CAA, the source told me that someone was not acting in an official capacity for the agency. All of the coverage that Lonely Girl 15 got, and its explosion in popularity, can be attributed to its uniqueness, sure, but also for it being featured on the YouTube front page.[16])

The "Will It Blend?" videos were popular before being featured, but became insanely popular after, especially once Digg got behind their iPhone video. The effects of both led to the company's CEO being invited on *The Tonight Show with Jay Leno*. This was then followed by media appearances that included *The Today Show*, as well as on the Discovery Channel and the History Channel. Like in the case of Lonely Girl 15, being featured on the YouTube front page allowed Blendtec to access opportunities they otherwise would not have had to grow their audience further.

So to say that "Will It Blend?" went viral organically, passed on from viewer to viewer on its own, isn't true. It's also unclear what the impact on sales has been for the company. Nate Hirst said, "To date the sales of the product you see in the videos is up 1,000 percent."[17] I don't doubt that. They're great videos, it's a great campaign, and it seems like a great product; but that number is also a bit vague. Like my Dad always says, "a thousand percent of nothing is still nothing." It doesn't mean much unless we have something to compare it to; but like all of these companies, getting actual numbers to discuss is almost impossible (and where we find an information gap, others find an opportunity).

## 2008: ZAPPOS

In 2008, marketers and the media moved on to Zappos, the awesome online shoe store where they actually have shoes in the size you need. Zappos was featured in Brian Solis's *Engage*, Liana Evans's *Social Media Marketing: Strategies for Engaging In Facebook, Twitter, and Other Social Media*, Joel Comm's *Twitter Power*, Dave Evans and Jack McKee's *Social Media Marketing: The Next Generation of Business Engagement*, Bernie Brennan and Lori Schafer's *Branded!: How Retailers Engage Consumers with Social Media and Mobility*, and Tamar Weinberg's *The New Community Rules: Marketing on the Social Web*, in addition to countless other blog posts, videos, e-books, and other "social media" pornography.

How did the marketers find out about Zappos? The Twitter Suggested User List. As Ev Williams, former CEO of Twitter, explained to me,

> *The suggested user list was created to address the "blank timeline problem." I.e., people would sign up for Twitter, be greeted with a blank timeline and have no clue what to do next. Our idea was to build a great way to discover accounts, based on who/what you were interested in, which we've since built a lot of. But at the time, we needed to start somewhere and wanted to do something quickly. So, we decided to try an experiment to see if we provided accounts we knew were good but randomly selected and totally unpersonalized (after all, we don't know anything about people when they first sign up)*

*would it be enough to give people the gist of what Twitter is about and make them more likely to stick.*[18]

@Zappos (CEO Tony Hsieh's account) received the same big boost in followers that I, Gary Vaynerchuk, CNN, Ashton Kutcher, Shaq, Mashable, JetBlue, Dell, and many, many others got from being featured on the list. That increase in follower count led to the marketers taking notice of these and the other companies featured there and declaring them to be "social media" success stories. This was despite the fact that not all was what it seemed concerning those with the inflated follower counts. As Ev added, "An unintended consequence was the accounts on the early list got inflated follower counts, because people didn't specifically select them based on real interest. (I personally removed myself after a while, because I didn't see value in lots of people who didn't know who I was following me—also, I didn't figure I was probably that interesting.)" He continued, "We talked about updating follower counts to reflect only active users, which I think would have good for the system, although not good for a lot of egos."

The difficulty in proclaiming Zappos to be a "social media" success story is that the CEO himself, Tony Hsieh, has said things in interviews such as "since we're not looking at them ['social media' platforms] as marketing channels, we aren't measuring marketing ROI."[19] I asked Tony what he thought of Zappos being described as a social media success story, and he answered, "Our goal is to build personal, emotional connections with people, whether they are customers, employees, or our vendors/business partners. Twitter (for example) just happens to be one way to do it, but so is the telephone. Nobody cites Zappos as a 'telephone success story,' so I think it's a bit strange to cite Zappos as a 'social media' success story."[20]

Corina Craig at Zappos also mentioned to me that Tony hates the term "social media." Tony elaborated, "I think the term puts the focus on the method instead of the intent. Ultimately what really matters is connecting with people, and most companies haven't figured out how to do that by telephone yet."

When Amazon purchased Zappos, the marketers stopped talking about the company completely.

## 2009: DELL

In 2009, Chris Brogan and many other marketers moved on from Zappos to Dell, where they happily reported that Dell made $3 million using Twitter.[21] How exactly Dell did so is unclear, and they declined to comment for this book.

To provide some background on Dell's Twitter presence, @DellOutlet joined Twitter on May 1, 2007. When the Twitter Suggested User List rolled out in 2009, it brought their account over 1.5 million followers. Today, they're at 1,577,174.

As actor and comedian Michael Ian Black told me about the followers he gained from the Suggested User List, "I have an artificially inflated follower count as a result of that initial suggestion list that Twitter put out early on. There's absolutely no other explanation for why I have the amount of followers that I have. As of this interview I have a gorgeous 1,682,845 following me. Of which I'm assuming 95 percent to 96 percent either aren't on Twitter anymore or do not have any idea they're following me or know who I am."[22]

Since coming off the list, the @DellOutlet account's growth has been minimal, if not nonexistent. By the end of 2009, after the $3 million sales figure was released into the wild that summer, Dell said they had made $6.5 million in sales through Twitter.[23] Of the original $3 million, they attributed $2 million to Twitter, and $1 million to direct sales made through Twitter. The most important number to pay attention to though is: 13,400,000. I'll tell you why in a minute. But note that in *none* of the posts Dell rolled out to talk about any of this, nor in any of the posts done by most of the tech blogs like Mashable or by the marketers, was the Twitter Suggested User List mentioned. JetBlue, when I interviewed their reps, didn't mention it, but bragged about how many Twitter followers they had. (They admitted to having been on the list only when asked.)

So, instead of mentioning this vital piece of information, you got overly cheery half-truths, like this, posted on Dell's blog in June of 2009:

> So I started tweeting more regularly and doing more Twitter-exclusive offers, which created more buzz and helped us to grow our follower base (we're now over 600,000). Our followers responded by re-tweeting @DellOutlet messages to their followers, and our numbers rose even more. . . . @DellOutlet is getting close to the top 50 most followed Twitter users according to TwitterCounter, sharing the stage with brands like @Zappos.

Not mentioned in the story of their meteoric rise? The Suggested User List.

Also, $3 million may sound like a lot of money to us, but to Dell, it's nothing. They had $61.10 billion of revenue in 2009. And Dell's 2010 fiscal year revenue was $52 billion, meaning they lost a pile of money the year following their "social media success." When that last bit of news came out, the "Dell as a social media success story" myth was also quietly dropped by the marketers.

Now let's assume for a second that Dell was indeed directing people from Twitter to purchase through their Web site—drawing on the effectiveness of coupons, and the emotional investment people have in their brand. It's reasonable to assume that some customers are going to act on it and maybe make a purchase or two. How many of them and whether that's worth the investment in time and resources on Dell's part, is a big question. And considering their alleged Twitter earnings were a drop in the bucket, and the cost in time, energy, and money of maintaining a high-profile account can be substantial, it looks doubtful. (The fact that Dell hasn't said much of anything about Twitter in a long time supports this theory.)

That brings us back to the magic number of 13,400,000. That's the number of search results you'll find in Google for posts and Web sites that talk about Dell's "social media success story" involving Twitter. The amount of good publicity generated from the legion of tech blogs— that don't bother to do any fact checking—not to mention the countless marketers, Cyber Hipsters, analysts, and others who parrot those tech and "social media" blogs, is arguably worth more than any revenue Dell brought in by using Twitter. In the end, this was just a big PR stunt for Dell. And it worked out well, but to be clear: It was never a "social media success story."

## 2010: OLD SPICE

In 2010, the marketers left Dell behind and then climbed aboard the Old Spice bandwagon, declaring it to be yet another "social media success story." It began with an ingeniously scripted and edited thirty-second video, featuring actor and former pro athlete Isaiah Mustafa as the Old Spice Man. Suddenly the man you can smell like was everywhere. How good was this ad campaign? Viewers everywhere recalled seeing it during the Super Bowl. As Dean McBeth, former senior digital strategist at Wieden + Kennedy—the advertising agency that set up the campaign—told me, "The original spot, 'The Man Your Man Could Smell Like,' debuted Super Bowl weekend to Old Spice fans first (YouTube, Facebook and Twitter). A very strategic search buy placed it in the wrap-up conversation around Super Bowl commercials and a full-out media blitz the following week still has most people believing that it was in fact a Super Bowl commercial."[24] (And although the commercial was *not* a Super Bowl ad, the Old Spice man saw heavy promotion during the Olympics.)

That summer when the Old Spice "social media" campaign rolled out, it heavily featured Mustafa responding to tweets at @OldSpice, via custom-made videos that were shot, edited, and uploaded as replies the very same day the original tweets were posted. It was an incredibly smart marketing campaign, put on by Wieden + Kennedy and backed by Proctor & Gamble's nearly limitless funds. Those Old Spice video replies included responses to celebrities like Ryan Seacrest, Ashton Kutcher, Ellen Degeneres, Apolo Ohno, and Cyber Hipsters Kevin Rose, Biz Stone, and Guy Kawasaki. It shouldn't come as any surprise that out of the two hundred or so videos created for the Old Spice "social media" campaign, most of the views were associated with these videos, as well as the ones made for popular online communities like 4Chan and Reddit.[25]

Since P&G saw a rise in sales that corresponded with the online portion of the advertising campaign,[26] it must have been a "social media success story"—right?

Not even close. First of all, the campaign was supported by a heavy (and expensive) television presence. Dean said, "Not only was the Old Spice Man becoming a pop culture phenomenon, the man himself, Isaiah Mustafa had won the hearts of the ladies on just about every daytime talk show you can name. Including *Oprah, The Ellen Show,* G4TV, ESPN, the list goes on."[27] The Old Spice Man was a great advertising campaign, certainly, but given his offline omnipresence—prior to the campaign as an actor, and during the campaign—not to mention the reliance on established celebrities, it looks doubtful. It was a masterful use of the Web, by a well-organized team, using an omnipresent character that people loved. "Social media" was a small component.

More to the point: After the marketer hysteria died down, reports started to come out that found Old Spice sales for that year were mostly driven by offline advertising and coupon sales.

So much for "social media" magic.

If you want further proof that you can't credit "social media" for Old Spice's success in 2010, look no further than Cisco's "Ted from Accounting" campaign. Cisco's Old Spice clone didn't have the offline media support, or the celebrity component, but attempted to mirror the Old Spice online campaign in every other way—and failed horribly.[28] Commenting on the success, and Cisco's attempt to mimic the Old Spice Man campaign, Dean added, "The response campaign [for Old Spice, on Twitter] was a perfect storm and isn't something you can replicate just by doing video responses in social media. The amount of awareness media, the organic acceleration of conversation and video views, the love generated for Isaiah Mustafa, and the persona of the Old Spice guy. All of the variables lined up perfectly. Plus, we had a huge amount of leverage pre-responses. Celebrity, media, and other online influencers had already been talking about Old Spice and we were able to effectively leverage that word of mouth. To our knowledge, nobody knew who Ted was."[29]

The marketers' spin will never stop. But it's not just the marketers and Cyber Hipsters who are stretching the truth. It's the companies that run these platforms, too. Just ask Facebook.

CHAPTER THIRTEEN

# KIA AND FACEBOOK SITTING IN A TREE . . .

**THE COMPANIES WHO RUN** these platforms have just as much to gain by spreading bullshit as the marketers do. It may be free to make a Facebook page, but that doesn't mean running your campaign on that platform is going to be.

If you're, say, Kia Motors America, you've got millions at your disposal to throw at a marketing campaigns and to show your superiors, who have mandated you to have some kind of social media initiative, that you can use Facebook just as well as anyone else. Or, more likely, your advertising agency (who is on retainer and gets paid regardless of your success or failure) told you having a Facebook page was a good idea. I've got an equally good idea: Take a dump on your account manager's lawn in the dead of night. It'll be just as productive as sinking money into Facebook.

These initiatives aren't cheap. Neither is the fine you're going to pay if you get caught taking my advice. "Social media" campaigns can run upwards of $200,000 to operate.[1] Of course, you're not Kia. You have a smaller budget to work with. So, sure it's "free" to start a Facebook page, but how are you going to let people know about it? Are you paying someone to update that page? Is it an intern, and if so, could they be doing something else more productive? If it's a staff member, how experienced are they at running a Facebook campaign? And what are you getting from having that Facebook page that you can't get from your Web site? Memo to corporations: Putting Facebook icons on your ads or telling people to "find you on Facebook" is probably one of the dumbest things you'll ever do. There's no proof anyone cares.[2]

There's also the cost of using the Web, business expenses, and if you're selling stuff through there, you have inventory to manage and ship. So yes, the start-up cost is nonexistent, but that rarely translates into something you can make money from without putting in a lot of time, energy, and resources for what could be a potentially small payoff.

I'm not writing off Facebook. There are very narrow and small cases where using it could work, but they're rare and like with YouTube, there are many other factors involved with that success that need to be considered carefully. The only parties who consistently benefit from a sustained Facebook campaign are the people running it for you (like an advertising agency or PR firm) and Facebook. In the run-up to Facebook's IPO, Sheryl Sandberg said this about the benefit to Facebook of having small businesses use their service: "Sharing activity drives advertising revenue for us. It's important for big businesses and brands, but also really important for small businesses. A lot of them do advertise and if they continue to grow, they will [advertise]. Even if they're not advertising, [they're] driving users and driving engagement." In other words: Your presence on Facebook benefits them, not you.[3] Eighty-five percent of Facebook's revenue comes from advertising and the illusion that people use their Web site and interact with things while they're there, even though what people are doing once they're in Facebook is vaguely defined. It appears Facebook is counting you liking something elsewhere but not going to the main Facebook.com site as an active user, which seems pretty shady. That's why Facebook does things like charge you more money in placing an advertisement if you're sending people from Facebook, but charge you less for keeping those people there. They benefit by keeping you there and getting your customers to interact with their stuff.

## INSIDE FACEBOOK'S REALITY DISTORTION FIELD

I don't know if you can attribute Kia's first quarter 2011 sales success to their Facebook efforts. Really. I don't. Which I guess is good because no one else can, either. Remember when I mentioned how analysts state the obvious? Well, when you start seeing headlines in *The Wall Street Journal*, fueled by reports by analysts like Forrester, that say, "Facebook Won't Become E-Commerce Force," you should take notice. Although analysts do make things up to sell more reports (see Chapter 11), most of them state the obvious because it's a safe financial bet to do so. If they continue to make stuff up, other businesses won't buy their reports.

But that *Wall Street Journal* headline didn't stop Facebook from releasing a marketing case study that said otherwise. Of course they did. The leading source of revenue for Facebook is advertising, and they want to make sure they hold on to that $3.7 billion they generated in revenue in 2011 to keep all their shareholders happy. In order to protect that number, Facebook has also started a major push to get small businesses to advertise on their platform. And guess what their focus is on? If you guessed, "educating" small business owners," you know what? You're really good at guessing what I'm going to say. (If you're going to spend so much time in my head, you better start paying rent.)

In 2011, Facebook put out a case study that included the following results to prove that Kia's advertising campaign on their platform worked:

- The Soul sustain campaign led to a 13-point increase in awareness for Kia's Soul, according to a study conducted by media research firm, The Nielsen Company.
- According to Nielsen, 14 percent of individuals said their perception of the Kia brand improved after seeing the ad (a significant increase over the control group).
- The Premium Video Like Ads, including the names of friends who had already connected to Kia via "Friends of Connections" targeting, resulted in the highest engagement rate for the campaign.
- There are now over 89,000 people who are part of the Kia Soul Facebook community, which means the brand can reach over 31 million friends of those fans with Friends of Connections Targeting.

Since anything Facebook does is news for some depressing reason, the notion that Kia's Facebook Fan Page translated to sales has spread. I'm not going to go so far as to say that Kia Motors America is wasting its time on Facebook. It's too difficult to know. But most businesses are, often because they're surrendering traffic and attention that should be going to their own Web sites and giving it to Facebook instead.

Unless there's something to be gained by being on Facebook, you shouldn't have a presence there. All traffic and attention should always be focused on one Web site—one that you own. If people like what you do, and you've made it easy for them to find you, they'll pass it on using Facebook. So there's no point in having a Facebook page just to have one. Your presence there is redundant.

And despite what a marketer or Facebook might tell you, "liking" something doesn't necessarily translate into new sales. In fact, a little more than half of the people who like a Facebook page are usually customers. (The same study, released by Boston-based consulting firm

Chadwick Martin Bailey, also said that half of the people who "like" a page are more likely to buy from that company, but if they were customers already, that doesn't really say much.) There's also no way of knowing how often fans are visiting the page and seeing the updates in their newsfeed. Especially because the average post only lasts for twenty minutes or so in the newsfeed before it's buried by something else (something more important if it's coming from that person's friends). Half of Facebook's active users log in once a day. Depending on when you post something, how many friends they have, and when they log in, it's possible that they'll never see your post. This is especially likely if you have an advertising agency or outside vendor only updating the Facebook page during business hours, when most people are at work. They could be a "fan" and never visit your page (and that seems often to be the case as it's incredibly murky, by Facebook's own definition to determine what exactly makes an "active" user). There's no way of knowing and Facebook isn't saying anything beyond general stuff like "50 percent of our active users log on to Facebook in any given day" and "There are over 900 million objects that people interact with pages, groups, events, and community pages."[4]

That's why "awareness" and "engagement" are bad metrics. Besides being vague, there's just no way of really knowing if someone is seeing what you do on Facebook (or other platforms). It's a lot like traditional advertising, nobody really knows for sure if the ads work, but if business is good they'll credit the ads. And if business is bad they'll blame them and say they're ineffective. (Perhaps not coincidentally, Facebook is pushing the perception that ads on their platform should be viewed and measured in the same vague way television ads are.) For every statement we see indicating that one Facebook fan equals twenty visits to your Web site over the course of a year (as reported by Experian Hitwise), we get another that says the more fans you have, the fewer unique views your Facebook page gets (according to analytics company Page Leveler).[5]

Bottom line? Facebook is running an elaborate shell game because almost all of their revenue comes from fooling people into thinking advertising with them is effective, even though it's seemingly not.

So if most of the people who are becoming a fan of yours on Facebook are already fans *off* of Facebook, wouldn't it just make more sense to focus your attention on building traffic to your Web site and acquiring new customers through stuff that actually works? Like SEO?

I submit to you, my friends, that it does.

And if you're thinking "Is SEO bullshit?" I'll defer to the only person I trust on that subject, Roberta Rosenberg, who is the CEO of MGP Direct: "No, it's not bullshit. It's not magical or mysterious, either. What it represents at its core is the language and mind-set of the searcher at any given moment in time. While keywords, phrases, and relevant content remain key here, there are behind-the-scenes infrastructures that can help or hurt search engine rankings. Relevant content packaged smartly is the hallmark of effective SEO."[6] And given that most traffic for nonnews Web sites still comes from search engines, and that probably won't change as long as the Web stays in its current incarnation, it's worth looking into SEO. That said, I'm not an expert on it, and there's just as much bullshit surrounding SEO as there is social media, so the only thing I can recommend here is caution, plenty of research, and to make sure you get testimonials and case studies from the people you're looking into hiring. If at all possible, talk to their current and former customers. (Also: Don't hire an SEO consultant, or anyone for that matter, until you've exhausted all your free options.)

## THE KIA CASE STUDY

Return on investment *isn't* everything. Getting people to learn more about you *is* important. But getting that exposure and turning it into something sustainable is insanely difficult. Think of it this way: 70 percent of views on YouTube, according to YouTube's official press page, come from outside of the United States. If you make your money doing live performances (as most performers do, particularly through merchandise sales at those live events), it doesn't matter how big you are in Bulgaria. Ditto for small businesses. Unless you can sell something to your friends overseas, it doesn't really matter if they like you or not when you're trying to make rent each month.

"Awareness" and "engagement," as they're used by champions of social media, don't mean anything. They're meaningless metrics made up by marketers. Show me a company that brags about the number of likes their expensive social media campaign generated, and I'll show you a company trying to justify the money they wasted to unhappy shareholders.

This is what Pepsi did after the failure of their Pepsi Refresh social media campaign. Instead of advertising during the (then) most-watched television event in history, they opted to spend $20 million on the social media–based Pepsi Refresh project.[7][8] In the face of falling sales and sagging brand status, Pepsi CEO Indra Nooyi pointed to the number of likes Pepsi Refresh received as a sign that it was worth the expenditure.[9]

In the case of big companies and big brands, ROI may not be everything. But for the rest of us? It's the only thing that matters because for a lot of small businesses, artists, and entrepreneurs, if you don't make money, you can't keep doing what you're doing. It's as simple as that. Even some of the big brands most commonly associated with social media admit that it isn't viewed as a money-making tool. A JetBlue representative told me, "We don't look at our 'social media' strategy in terms of profit. We consider the value of being able to communicate with our customers via 'social media' as something that can't be defined in dollars and cents. The usefulness of being able to push information out to a large number of people in a short amount of time, and to reach our customers in a voice that is accessible, is invaluable."[10]

But here's the thing, the stated objective from the Facebook Kia case study was, "Drive sales and consideration for the Kia Soul, and build a brand community."[11] The "build a brand community" part no one cares about. It doesn't mean anything other than "get a Facebook page where people can hang out, so Facebook can collect more information about them to sell to their partners." So if major corporations don't see their "social media" presence as a way to make money, then why do Facebook and the marketers continue to frame things in that way for the rest of us? I also have questions about the "success" Facebook cites in their Kia marketing case study: "There are now over 89,000 people who are part of the Kia Soul Facebook community, which means the brand can reach over 31 million friends of those fans with Friends of Connections."

That's hypothetical, if not plain delusional. Hasn't Facebook said that only half of their "active" users check in every day? How many of those 89,000 fans are "active users"? What if those fans have decided to hide Kia's updates from their newsfeed or simply ignore those updates? Is Facebook measuring by clicks, or by something else? Either way, numbers like this are optimistic at best and manipulative at worst. We assume when we hear things like, "Kia Motors America reports a 13 percent increase in awareness about the Soul" that this leads to sales, but there's no data to back that up. Even Kia's vice president of marketing, Michael Sprague, expressed doubt to *The Wall Street Journal* that advertising on Facebook has led to new vehicle sales.

Ditto when you read stuff like this from AllFacebook.com, the "unofficial Facebook resource":

Kia executives have good reason to be thrilled with the results of their campaign. They include:

- The premium video like ads, including the names of friends who had already connected to Kia via "Friends of Connections" targeting, resulted in the highest engagement rate for the campaign.[12]

Sounds impressive, right? And Kia's sales have jumped 37 percent in the first quarter of 2011, but how much of this is because of likes on Facebook? The evidence that the Kia campaign worked in the Facebook case study was based entirely on Nielsen finding a 13 percent increase in "awareness" and that 14 percent of the people they surveyed said the campaign had improved their perception of Kia. What is 13 percent and 14 percent of the 89,000 Facebook fans? Thirteen percent is 11,570 fans. Let's imagine every single one of those 11,570 fans decided to buy a new car in 2011 and went with the Kia Soul for $13,300 (without any additional options, and not counting whatever the dealership mark up is), that would be about $15 million in revenue for Kia. Not too shabby, but . . . Kia in 2010 made $2.02 billion in revenue (converted from South Korean Won at the January 2011 exchange rate). So $15 million is nice, but not a huge dent. It's actually .7 percent of Kia's revenue.

And how much do you suppose Kia is spending on Facebook advertisements, maintaining their Facebook pages, and paying staff to maintain that page (in addition to operating other Facebook-related activities)? JetBlue didn't disclose how much they spent on their social media efforts. Many of the companies I talked to don't. In Kia Motor America's Case, they've hired the Zeno Group (an Edelman PR firm) to run their Twitter and Facebook presence. Given that the Zeno Group works with big brands like AT&T, Pizza Hut, and Discovery Communications, I can't imagine they're cheap. (The Zeno Group did not return my calls and e-mails requesting comment.) So is Kia Motors of America spending more than they are taking in? We only know how much Pepsi spent because they wanted the press attention that went with ditching the 2010 Super Bowl, and how much Dell allegedly made off Twitter in 2009 for the same reasons. But it seems all of these companies don't look at their social media initiatives as revenue generators; instead they rely on squishy things like "engagement," "community," "awareness," and "listening" to justify the expense.

Yet . . . marketers consistently frame "social media" as a driver for a financial return on investment. Is "social media" in reality a loss leader for them? And if so, what about the rest of us who can't afford to burn that kind of money on efforts meant to draw people in and sell them on other things?

Here's the big question: Given all this evidence, who are these case studies being rolled out for? It's always the marketers who seem to hear about them outside of the Facebook.com/Marketing portal, and all of them have a vested interest in reporting positive news on that front. If they don't, they're going to look dated to potential clients; if they do, they strengthen their position by appearing to be "Thought Leaders." Is Facebook aware of how marketers spread distorted information to these companies and in Facebook helping the marketers do so? Are these case studies only being shown to big corporations because they can afford to piss away their already allocated marketing dollars on Facebook? And if that's the case, what does that mean for those small businesses, artists, and entrepreneurs who don't have the money to burn and are looking to replicate the same effects in "brand awareness"?

Spoiler Alert: It ain't good.

I'm not going to dispute that Facebook likes and fans *could* lead to sales. Facebook, for already established media companies (i.e. The New York Times, Yahoo!, and CNN), has brought those sites more traffic. That much is true. But, I do question how many sales likes and fans can bring, and whether the amount of money, time, effort, and energy that's put into those Facebook campaigns would be better utilized elsewhere for those companies and individuals without multi-million dollar marketing budgets. That decision rests with you. Everyone is different, but remember: What works for a big brand and a celebrity *does not* work for the rest of us. Unfortunately, all of these marketers are gunning for the big corporate and government marketing budgets, not yours. So despite what advice, which seems like it's geared toward you, says, following the lead of a company like Kia—without their resources and with the uncertainty of success—is a great way to put your emerging business or creative project into bankruptcy.[13]

When a corporation scores a "social media success," it is often the equivalent of scoring an empty-net goal in hockey. The company is either already doing well, as Kia was, so they can claim whatever they want and use the earnings to support it. Or they're using meaningless metrics, like how many times a free app has been downloaded, to support their alleged success story. Like an empty-net goal, neither approach requires much effort, because no one is there to stop you from scoring. In none of these social media "successes" did anyone covering the story do any digging, accepting what they were told by these companies and the marketers at face value.

This wouldn't be the first time marketers used a major company as an example for why people should use new services, either. In Chris Brogan's *Trust Agents*, he used General Motors as a case study for crowdsourcing. But you're not General Motors, either. (Although, if you pay your taxes, you technically own part of them.)

But don't call Chris, Seth, and the other marketers out on stuff like that. You wouldn't like them when they're angry. You'll find proof of that in the next chapter.

## CHAPTER FOURTEEN

# HOW MARKETERS, CYBER HIPSTERS, AND OTHERS DEAL WITH THEIR CRITICS (HINT: NOT WELL)

CHRIS BROGAN FACED heavy criticism from fellow "social media" marketers and the anti-"social media" crowd for holding this Google+ Webinar—and rightfully so.

The most important part of Brogan's response to the mutiny he faced among his fellow marketers, for our purposes, was this: "I'm not selling to [author and marketing strategist] Geoff Livingston. I'm not selling to [social media professional and blogger] Danny Brown. I'm not selling to all the people whose panties are all in a bunch because I've chosen to sell information on how to use Google+ for your business. You're not my buyer."[1]

He's right. "Social media" and "social media" skeptics aren't his buyer. But that doesn't justify taking advantage of people who don't know any better by selling them bullshit. Unfortunately, Brogan's response to criticism, in this instance, heavily mirrors the kind of response you'll see whenever marketers and other Cyber Hipsters are called out. In addition to calling you a dinosaur, they'll use faulty logic to justify their actions—sort of like an arsonist who burns down your house because he thought you needed a new one. When those tactics fail, they will react with an all-out assault—on you, your family, everything you do—in the hopes that it'll distract people and take the heat off of them.

When Tim O'Reilly was called out by Andrew Keen in his book, *The Cult of the Amateur*, for pushing a narrative that best serves the agenda of his business interests, O'Reilly replied by saying to the Dutch Public Broadcasting VPRO program, *Backlight*, "I find, Andrew Keen's, his whole pitch, I think he was just pure and simple looking for an angle, to create some controversy and sell a book, I don't think there's any substance whatever to his rants."[2] Lawrence Lessig, who received a beating from Keen in the book, replied with a 3,600-word response to Keen on his blog, and then the creation of a Wiki for people to pinpoint errors made in the book (my favorite entry of which involves this terribly punny line: "Keen has a less than keen understanding of economic value."). Lessig then attacks Keen's logic by comparing Michael Jacksons to Iron Maidens[3] (or more commonly known as: Comparing apples to oranges).

He points to Google:

> Take Google, for example, the economic paragon of a truly successful Web 2.0 media company. With a market cap of approximately $150 billion, the Silicon Valley company took in $6.139 billion in revenue and $1.465 billion in profits in 2005. Telling is the fact that unlike companies such as Time Warner or Disney that create and produce movies, music, magazines, and television, Google is a parasite; it creates no content of its own . . . . In terms of value creation, there is nothing there apart from its links . . . . Why stop at Google? Why not attack, for example, the creators of phone books. They too are simply "parasites" "creat[ing] no content of [their] own." FedEx doesn't make the stuff in the box, they just bring it to you efficiently. This argument is ridiculous. Improving the efficiency of access creates value.[4]

We're going to sidestep the fact that "improving the efficiency of access creates value" is almost Rumsfeldian, in that it's a needlessly complicated way of saying nothing. But of course, FedEx and the phonebook aren't Google. They're all very different things involving entirely different mediums. Sadly this is pretty much what the marketers, Cyber Hipsters, and others do when you call out their favorite service or platform. "If you're going to ban Twitter, why don't you ban the phone, too?" I swear I saw that said more than once when the government of the United Kingdom mentioned the idea of censoring "social media" services in the wake of the riots in London during the Summer of 2011.[5] Unfortunately, Maslow's hammer seems to come standard in the response toolbox for these parties. As I mentioned before with the Cyber Hipsters, if they see something is true in their respective industries, then they reason that it must be true for all industries. And even then I have my doubts because aside from a small handful of self-taught wiz kids, a lot of these guys came from good colleges like Stanford. That ain't cheap to attend. That's why you get broad, hilariously off-base comments like, "the cost of creating content is approaching zero." It's true in software, but not so much for anything else. So that sound you hear whenever things like this are said? It's what's left of Abraham Maslow trying to escape his grave and feast on the flesh of the living.

Whenever someone disagrees with these people, they will almost always reach for the dinosaur defense. Jeff Jarvis used to be the king of calling everyone and anyone, especially those that disagreed with him, dinosaurs. Do a Google site search for buzzmachine.com and "Dinosaurs," and you can see this in action. As Jarvis once said, "You don't have to be old to roar like a dinosaur."[6]

When asked by Keen and his publisher to debate him on the issues he raised, Jeff said of Andrew Keen's book *The Cult of the Amateur*, "The problem is that Keen's book is the worst of link bait. It's link whoring. Or should I say talk-show prostitution? It's frilly lace tempting those who want so much to dismiss this change. He tries to push every Internet button he can. Like others, Keen wants to be the contrarian's contrarian. But that only makes him a double negative. It makes him a curmudgeon, a conservative trying to hold onto the past, a mastodon growling against the warm wind of change."[7]

In his reply to Keen, Jeff missed an important point—namely, that although *The Cult of the Amateur* was not a perfect book (as Keen admits), Keen was right on one important thing: In championing "user generated content," it destroys the credibility of legitimate experts. And marketers exploit the loss of real experts to the fullest, remaking themselves as "experts" in fields that don't exist. (A theme we'll pick up again in the next chapter.)

I'm a fan of Jeff Jarvis, although there's little we agree on. And to Jeff's credit, he's backed off on this sort of name-calling. I asked him about the dinosaur defense, and he told me he's stopped using the term. He added, "The other thing I recanted, or tried very hard to, not always easy, but I tried very hard to recant was the notion of saying 'This group doesn't get it.' I was guilty of that, and dinosaur was the shorthand for that. I've confessed my sin and recanted that because the truth is: No one gets it. I don't get it. And by saying someone else doesn't get it would put me in the position of saying that I do. My point is bigger in that none of us get it. I think we're in the early part of this change [brought about by the Internet] and we ain't seen nothing yet."

I agree with Jeff on this point, and I appreciate that he's moved away from this sort of disparagement. Unfortunately, where Jeff has stopped, legions of professional and amateur marketers who have appeared since the recession began to use this line of thinking to bully people that disagree with them.

## ATTACK & DISTRACT

If you were to look over the comments left on my posts at Forbes concerning Mashable's "coverage" of Trey Pennington's death, you would have found social media marketers almost exclusively using a tactic I call "Attack and Distract." It's the same tactics Jeff Jarvis, Lawrence Lessig, and Tim O'Reilly used to deal with Andrew Keen's book, and how Chris Brogan responded to his critics. You know why stuff like this goes on? Because the Internet and the Web are filled with the kind of people you meet in high school: superficial, arrogant, quick to assume, quicker to blame, and full of sass. In other words? My kind of people. Unfortunately, my kind of people can be really annoying, especially when they're selling bad, misleading, and potentially dangerous information. So it's important to understand how Attack and Distract works so you can diffuse it.

### Shallow Relationships

Everyone is your friend on the Internet until you say something they don't like. Just Ask Malcolm Gladwell.

Since *The Tipping Point* came out, Internet marketers have pushed the ideas presented in that book relentlessly while praising Gladwell. That was until February 2011, when Gladwell wrote a piece on the *New Yorker's News Desk* blog called "Does Egypt Need Twitter."[8] Gladwell's argument was that the vehicle behind the message wasn't as important as the message and its origins. In other words, how the people in Egypt were coordinating their protests didn't matter, what mattered was that they were protesting and why they were protesting. This is a continuation of an argument Gladwell started in his *New Yorker* piece, "Small

Change: Why the Revolution Will Not Be Tweeted." There he stated that activism doesn't need "social media" to occur, and that, while the Web creates "weak ties," offline ties that are useful, strong, and organized are needed for anything to really happen.[9]

I agree with the broader points that Gladwell is making: The use of things like Twitter and Facebook are overhyped and are often distorted, as I've laid out for you. You're seeing the first wired generation take out their frustrations about the mess the world is in using the tools they grew up with. The fact that they're using Twitter and Facebook is incidental—to them. But as Evgeny Morozov points out in his book, *The Net Delusion*, the use of those tools is a big deal to the older generations, particularly the baby boomers, because it fits into a narrow worldview that they've been using to explain revolutionary changes that have occurred since the Soviet Union collapsed.[10] But this stuff is beyond the scope of a marketing book. Maybe in the next book we can talk about it.

After Gladwell's Egypt piece ran, the fun started. Everyone whose business interests could be hurt by Gladwell's comments, from the founders of Twitter, to an investor in foursquare, down to Gladwell's former Internet marketer fans, proceeded to flip out. And these people flipped in the fashion of the Web: by insulting you, your argument, your credibility, with as little evidence as needed. Hence: Attack and Distract.

So, for instance:

+ Insults: The cofounders of Twitter told GigaOM's Liz Gannes that Gladwell's first piece was, "laughable," "absurd," "ludicrous," and "pointless."[11]

+ Attacks on the quality of your work: In Gladwell's case, that his piece was well written but offers nothing new or of substance. Which is a clever way to dismiss an argument, but does nothing to refute it.

+ The red herring: This is a deliberate attempt to evade the point being raised or cloud the issue. In his blog post on the matter, Chris Dixon, cofounder of Hunch and a personal investor in four-square, ducked answering whether or not Gladwell was right. Instead, Dixon suggested Gladwell didn't know what he was talking about because he doesn't use Twitter and that the Twitter Gladwell refers to isn't "the Twitter that I know."[12] Dixon then goes on to point out how the connections he made on Twitter have been useful for him. A lot of you may know the red herring better as the "Chewbacca Defense." (If you don't, google "Chewbacca Defense." You'll see what I mean.)[13]

+ Michael Jacksons to Iron Maiden (Apples To Oranges): Twitter cofounder Biz Stone, writing for *The Atlantic*, talked about the impact Twitter has had on Chinese politics on the "micro-level."[14] Specifically, Stone took issue with Gladwell, in his pieces on Egypt and the ineffectiveness of "social media" at large to bring about real change in the world, saying there needed to be a strong, organized, networked, offline movement with a central leader or leadership to enact real change. Stone argues that this is no longer the case because activists could do similar things via platforms like Twitter. But here's the problem: Contrary to Stone's claim, nothing has changed in China, and beyond a superficial level, and at the time of this writing, not much has changed in Egypt either.[15]

Comparing China to Egypt, and the actions of activists in those countries, is also a Michael Jackson to Iron Maiden approach, especially when you consider the role of Al-Jazeera in promoting the protests, and the minimal role of the Egypitan military in disrupting them, during the time of the protests. This is compared to China's authoritarian censorship over the media and their active military and police role in quelling protests. But by comparing the two, Stone tries to demonstrate that Gladwell's argument is wrong despite plenty of evidence to the contrary. It's also worth noting a few other facts here about Twitter and Biz Stone: 1. Biz Stone is no longer associated with Twitter and, much like Sean Parker, his role at the company and developing the service remains a mystery.[16] 2. Twitter is banned in China. 3. In January 2012 Twitter announced localized censorship of Tweets, meaning if a Chinese activist, using the service illegally in China, posts something, then other people in China can't see what they're posting, but Americans can.[17] So . . . I'm not quite sure anyone can make the argument that Twitter is helping to cause real change on the "micro-level" Stone was talking about. It's kind of hard to change the status quo when the people your messages were meant for can't even see them.

## SO IS THIS PEOPLE JUST BEING DEFENSIVE, OR SOMETHING ELSE?

I'm not so sure. The knee-jerk answer is that everyone mentioned in this part of the book has something they want to protect. If Chris Brogan had been called out over his Google+ Webinar by someone with a big enough platform, he would have lost a lot of money. In the case of Jeff Jarvis, Tim O'Reilly, and other Cyber Hipsters, it's a bit more complicated.

The reason was nicely summed up by Evgeny Morozov. "Left unchallenged, [Internet intellectuals] may succeed in convincing us that we do indeed inhabit the digital wonderland of their imagination."[18] But let me take it a step further: The Internet intellectuals (or Cyber Hipsters), marketers, analysts, and their friends have succeeded. The existence of the myth of "social media" is proof of that. And it's important that we start cleaning up the mess they've created. Now that you know how this group is going to fight you, you can prepare for it and fight them back with the truth. What's needed now is for us to take a more active approach in standing up to their misinformation, calling them out on it, and making sure the media outlets, among others, who feature these parties are holding them accountable and to the highest ethical standard. It's no longer acceptable to have, for instance, Pete Cashmore of Mashable.com writing op-eds for CNN where he's promoting companies he has business relationships with in those op-eds, as he's done numerous times.[19] These are practices that breed further misinformation and myths that will continue to do irreparable harm to small businesses, artists, and entrepreneurs.

This book is a tour of the bullshit factory. So far I've showed you a lot of the bullshit products that get released, how they came to dominate online marketing, and why they're bad news. Now let's take a closer look at how exactly the bullshit spreads.

# PART III
# HOW TO SELL BULLSHIT WITHOUT REALLY TRYING

---

"Whenever you're exposed to advertising in this country you realize all over again that America's leading industry is still the manufacture, distribution, packaging, and marketing of bullshit."
—*George Carlin, comedian and social critic*

## CHAPTER FIFTEEN

# HOW TO CREATE AND SPREAD BULLSHIT IN SEVEN EASY STEPS

**PARTICIPATING IN THE DISHONEST ABE,** the Asshole-Based Economy, is easy. Any asshole can do it. Over the next few chapters, I'm going to show you how the marketers make up bullshit and use it to position themselves as experts on it.

Most of the bullshit involving things like "social media," "big data," "The Cloud," and "Web 2.0" spreads in a pattern. It looks like this:

1. A new tech company launches.
2. The tech media and Cyber Hipsters then cover that start-up obsessively. Declarations about how that company, app, or product will "change the game" are made.
3. The marketers act on what's being reported, telling their clients to "get in early" on these "game changers" that can "disrupt" their industry. (Although this could be true, it rarely is. For every Facebook, there are countless FriendFeeds; services that have a lot of promise, but for a variety of reasons, just don't go anywhere or get bought by the richer competition.)

4. Marketers jumping onto these new platforms create buzzwords in an effort to try to carve out a market for themselves.

5. Analysts read what the marketers are saying and repackage it as their own. Once they've put a report together, the analysts sell that information to businesses at outrageously marked-up fees.

6. Corporations decide they have to jump in based on what the analysts are saying and set aside their marketing dollars.

7. The rest of the media covers what the corporations are doing and reports on it, creating a demand for the marketers' books, on a subject area they've mostly fabricated. If those books are successful—if they become *New York Times* bestsellers—those marketers can grab a nice chunk of the money these corporations have set aside.

## Step One: Cut a Hole in the Box

Spreading bullshit that furthers my or anyone's interests on the Web is easy. Now I'm going to show you how to create and spread a myth using the Web in seven easy steps. I would say something here like, "Please only use this information for good," but that's like letting someone buy an AK-47 and asking them to only use it for "hunting."

**STEP 1:** The Asshole Based Economy begins when someone fabricates an idea that's false, harmful, or intentionally misleading in order to further their own long-term interests. We call this bullshit. (Remember: It's one thing to package and sell information. That's fine. It's another to package and sell *bad* information to further your own interests that can harm others.)

Imagine that I have an interest in seeing the Dodgers move back to Brooklyn (even if it's about as likely to happen as purchasing a healthy meal at a Five Guys). I need to tell the world that *it is happening*. It is an inevitability, and one that you need to face. If you don't, you—as a baseball fan, as a Dodgers fan, as an Angelino, as a New Yorker—are going to be left behind. You're a dinosaur, and not the fun kind arenas overcharge children to see.

What I want is something that will benefit me, the way a nice payday from a corporation benefits a marketer specializing in "social media." In order to do that, I need to become an "expert" on this subject. If I play my cards right, I could even widen my field later and become an "expert" in the relocation of sports teams, which could land me some nice, high-paying consulting gigs and even speaking dates. Maybe even a book deal.

So, the first thing you have to do is establish your "expertise" in the field and begin to plant the seeds for the lie to grow. In the world of the Internet, this starts with self-declaration: I am an "expert," "guru," "rock star," "scientist," or my personal favorite, "a ninja." (If you have to call yourself a ninja, you're clearly not ready for the responsibility of being one.) In this instance, I'm going to start calling myself an "advocate" for Brooklyn—for the positive impact that it would have both on the team and city. The reason for going with "advocate" over "expert" is simple. There's no easy, concise way to say "I'm an expert on relocating the Los Angeles Dodgers to Brooklyn." You could call yourself a "Dodgers Relo-cation Expert," but that's vague and not media friendly. "An advocate" is not ideal, either, but it's shorter and tells the whole story. Since being able to work the media is critical for you to succeed with the lie, that's closer to what you'll want to go with. Keep everything short, simple, and self-explanatory.

## Make Like a Kardashian

**Step 2:** It may not be free to produce (or to produce well), but the barriers to entry in posting something on the Web are close to zero. I know several people who were homeless, but that were using Twitter from public libraries. In that respect, being on the Web truly is equal opportunity. It's just too bad access is where the equality ends.

But you want to set yourself apart. You have to set up a professional-looking Web site. The more amateurish it looks, the less credibility you have. This is where money starts to become a factor. Your Web site has to look believable. The good news is that you can go to Wordpress.com and get a decent, but temporary, layout. The bad news is you now have to go and register a domain name for multiple years, and then pay Wordpress for the right to link your Wordpress.com blog with your newly purchased domain name. Google likes multiyear domain registrations. Shorter is better with a domain name, but you have to include your keywords, whatever you decide those to be. If you can't get them all into the domain name, get most of them. Something like Bringhomethebrooklyndodgers.com isn't great because of the length, but it also gives people an idea of what they're going to get. It comes down to experimentation on your part. The important thing is not to be too obvious or general.

Probably the best thing you can do when picking a domain name is to find something memorable. In the 1950s, Vincent X. Flaherty, for example, identified himself as an "advocate" to Walter O'Malley, former owner of the Brooklyn Dodgers.[1] Flaherty was a sportswriter, but made himself out to be a well-connected mover and shaker in the movement to bring a baseball team to Los Angeles. He wasn't. But if Flaherty were alive today, and he was trying to sell O'Malley on moving to Los Angeles, his Web site wouldn't play up that he's a journalist. It would play up that he's a mover and shaker. And in order to do that, he wouldn't have a domain name that was his name (although that's always a smart business decision); he would have something short and memorable—a domain name like LABaseball.com

Since you're just starting out and you don't have a lot to show off on the Web site, you should keep it nice and simple. Set up a blog, and start documenting the positive economic benefits the return of the Dodgers is going to have on Brooklyn. Yes, some work is going to be involved.

The good news is that the Web lets you "fake it until you make it,"[2] which is good because a convincing fraud can help you make the right connections you need to seem legit. The bad news? You're going to have a lot of competition until you build up some credibility. Every asshole in the world is doing the same thing you are because that's what marketers like the author of *No Bullshit Social Media* (an oxymoron if ever there was one) Jason Falls and "digital marketing visionary" Mitch Joel have told people to do. (Falls, it's worth noting, has taken the position that guys like me who complain about "social media" and marketers peddling it shouldn't because people are smart enough to know who is a fake and who isn't. But given the amount of money Facebook generates in advertising that is mostly ineffective and that Falls himself has said people need to fake it to make it, his statement seems kind of suspect. People *should* know better, but they don't. They don't because of the way information is spreading and being manipulated by select parties to further their own business interests at the expense of everyone else.)

Be that as it may, as my old history teacher Tommy Dames used to say after a tangent, talk to other people in the fields related to what you're talking about. I could talk to the borough president of Brooklyn, or a top sportswriter who covers the Dodgers. In fact, for the sake of illustrating how easy it is to establish yourself as an expert, I did exactly that. All it took was an e-mail request, and a phone call.

You can then take the information you collected and start putting it on your Web site, adding to it by finding secondary sources. So I could, for instance, pull books on the Dodgers and books about Brooklyn and publish some of the ideas they inspire, to fill the gap while I'm building up credibility.

And when you run out of material? Talk to people close to the issue you're pretending to be an expert on.

If you do all that? You're well on your way to becoming an expert yourself.

Don't worry about whether what you're writing is absolutely true. It looks like you've done your research, and that's what matters. The key is to keep digging. And if you're feeling really lazy, you can always hire an outsourcing firm or a couple of freelancers to collect the data and write about it for you on the blog. Either way, with sources to back up whatever it is that you're claiming, you *look* legit.

Now, you might be asking, "Well, doesn't doing all that research make you an expert then?"

On paper, it should. But the truth is never that simple. It really comes down to your depth of knowledge. Think, for example, about Chris Brogan's Webinar on enhancing your business's presence on Google+ and consider the facts: He claimed to spend 250 hours on the service. The service was twenty-four days old. He said businesses should get in early. Google was actively deleting business accounts and telling them to stay away. Related claims, like that he made Twitter a business staple in 2006, were also false. His "expertise" begins to look suspect.

We'd like to think we're good at spotting bullshit, but we're not. So the trick is to educate yourself, because the more that you know, the easier it'll be to spot bullshit in the wild. Although he was skeptical that we could ever stop the flow of bullshit because there were too many opportunities for it to be created, and "too much to be gained from it," Harry G. Frankfurt, professor emeritus of philosophy at Princeton University, told me, "Telling the truth and directing people's attention to it would certainly be salutary, and might succeed in making the bullshit around us a bit less effective, in making people less susceptible to falling for it. Poking fun at it might be especially effective, in humiliating the bullshitters and leading them to control their inclinations to it."[3]

I can assure you: The people who have real knowledge when it comes to social networks, their demographics, and their use aren't going to walk into a room and tell you that you need to post twice a day on Facebook, have a Twitter account, post videos on YouTube, and check in often on foursquare. The people who say that are bullshitting you.

The knowledgeable people are going to tell you which platform, *if any*, might be a good fit for you and your audience and figure out a way to best integrate it into what you do. You can tell the difference by asking a lot of questions about the stuff they claim to be knowledgeable of. As Professor Frankfurt pointed out in *On Bullshit*, "The production of bullshit is stimulated whenever a person's obligations or opportunities to speak about some topic exceed his knowledge of the facts that are relevant to that topic."[4]

This raises an interesting question that we should take a minute to address. Are any of these "social media" platforms actually useful?

# CHAPTER SIXTEEN
## AND THE ANSWER IS . . .

———————————

**STEP 3:** With your "well-sourced" Web site at the ready, and, if all goes well, an author page where you play up your credentials, you're now ready to join the exciting world of "social media."

Of course, "social media" is bullshit. But what about the platforms that are collectively referred to as "social media"? When it comes to spreading your message, are any of them useful?

Of the "Big Six," LinkedIn, foursquare, and Facebook are totally useless—useless, that is, for trying to advance yourself and spread the bullshit you've just created. LinkedIn serves a very specific purpose for people in the corporate and professional workforce, and for those people, it may be useful. But for our purposes, using LinkedIn is a waste of time. Especially when it comes to marketing and promoting yourself. You want a *receptive* audience, not an audience that considers "introductions" and e-mails from people they've barely talked to—at work or at a conference—a nuisance, on par with having a roommate who's really into marathon viewings of *Ice Road Truckers*.

And like with LinkedIn, Facebook also occupies that mostly useless zone. For friends and family? Sure. Go nuts! For marketing and promoting yourself? You really have to have a huge budget and a lot of time, energy, and resources to put into it, and even then, there are not many examples that involve a large, positive return on what was put into it, as you've seen. So while Facebook's platform may let us do interesting things with our friends and families, here it's a waste of time. And if you're still not convinced, ask GameStop, JCPenney, the Gap, Nordstrom, Banana Republic, and 1-800-FLOWERS how their Facebook stores are going. Hint: Not well. It turns out few to none of their millions of fans wanted to buy stuff through Facebook.[1]

As far as foursquare goes, Zzzzzzzzzz. Ok. I'm kidding, mostly, but about 4 percent of Americans use foursquare, and the rate of adoption for the service (at the time of this writing) has been pretty flat.[2] Which is a shame because you can do some exciting stuff with foursquare. I pressed a friend of mine, Michael Eliran, who works in the product-integration field as vice president of client services at Gamma Communications, to defend foursquare and show me a good use for it, and he gave me the following example:

> [An] example is what they are doing with Pepsi (and all their brands) at Von's supermarkets tied into the Von's store rewards card. They have linked consumers' foursquare account numbers to their Von's rewards card numbers (for consumers who opt-in). Since foursquare is a geo location–based service, they know when and where a consumer checks in. So if you check in at the gym a lot, they know that you are active or if you check-in early in the morning they know you are an early riser. So, through this program, when those consumers check-in at Von's, foursquare knows their habits and will serve special Pepsi offers to them while shopping, i.e., Tropicana orange juice for the early riser or Gatorade for the active gym-goer, and the consumer only needs to accept the coupon to have it instantly

*taken off their bill at check-out because the account is linked to their*
*rewards card number.*

Pretty cool, right? But here's the catch: So few people actually use foursquare that you could safely skip out on doing so and never know the difference. So while it may be worth the time, effort, and resources of the large corporations to try stuff like this out, for the rest of us with limited resources, foursquare shouldn't be at the top of the list for places to use them. (Although I will say this: Of the Big Six, foursquare is the closest to where all these services are heading, especially as more and more people are accessing these platforms from their smartphones and tablets. That's how most people around the world access Facebook. At the very least, it doesn't hurt to keep an eye on products and services like foursquare, even if I can't recommend using them. Foursquare just might wind up as the shareyourworld.com of its time.)

I use Tumblr. Mostly because I'm lazy, and when I started working on this book, I just didn't have time to write blog posts. Tumblr is good for sharing quick pieces of media, not just links but pictures, audio, and video. Where it falls flat though is that while it's incredibly easy for things to be shared on the platform, the service is incredibly ineffective when it comes to SEO and getting your material out to people *beyond* those who use it. Remember: You want to direct people to *one* central location, but that centralized location has to be easily found and indexed by Google, otherwise you just don't exist. That's why Google is so powerful. I've been using Tumblr since 2008. I like the service, but I would never recommend anyone start there. I hope that changes. But for now, search is too important to overlook, especially because it's one of the few ways to bring in traffic for whatever it is you're bullshitting about without getting a boost from a media outlet or celebrity. Most of the Tumblr blogs that have gone on to book deals took off for exactly the same reason that Chris Crocker's "Leave Britney Alone" video blew up: It served the business interests of the outlets posting about it. That's not exactly something that's going to work in your favor. You have better odds of sleeping with She-Hulk.

That leaves us with YouTube and Twitter. Here's the dirty little secret about YouTube: Unless the video is so bad it becomes good—and those videos are usually adopted by a Web community like 4Chan and Reddit before spreading to the corporate blogs—most videos that generate a lot of views are, not surprisingly, well produced. That means a lot of money was put into equipment, and even an editor or two was hired to make sure it didn't look like something you'd find in Kevin Federline's closet: crap. The overall talent of the people on camera is debatable, but the more likable and relatable someone is, the better their videos do. Oh, and did I mention yet that the average age of YouTube's audience is twelve- to seventeen-year-old boys?[3] That may be an advertiser's wet dream, but it's a producer's nightmare if that's not your audience.

So given all that, I say don't bother. YouTube is great to upload your videos and host them elsewhere, but for our purposes, that's about where the advantages end. No one is likely to see your video there anyway.

That leaves us with Twitter. I like Twitter, but Twitter sucks at a lot of things. For example, they want everyone to use the service from Twitter.com, but organizing and managing your friends on there is only slightly preferable to being water-boarded. That said, Twitter *is* good for connecting with strangers. And since many journalists and bloggers have a Twitter presence (disproportionately so, which is why you get so many Twitter-obsessed news stories despite the fact that so few people, comparatively speaking, actually use it), it's easy to contact them.[4] Twitter is also the only platform I mentioned here that allows you to follow and interact with anyone without any sort of friction. I've made a lot of great connections using the service, many of which have lead to jobs and other writing opportunities I wouldn't have had otherwise. But that's about where the positives for Twitter end (again, for our purposes). So out of all these platforms, the only one I can recommend even remotely considering wasting your time with is Twitter. And even then, be careful, it's good for connecting, not so much driving traffic or attention. Just ask any one of their unhappy advertising partners who find their promoted trending topics hijacked by comedians or an embarrassingly low click-through rate on their promoted tweets. (Notice a pattern forming here? In most cases, money spent on "social media" platforms is money wasted. You get a way better return on doing your own thing on your own Web site and doing things the old-fashioned way, but if you're going to use any of these platforms, you get better results by not spending any money at all. That's great for you, but really bad for all these "social media" companies, which is why it's their job to hype their numbers and mislead you when it comes to the results you'll get from making a sizable advertising investment with them.)

Let's get back to spreading bullshit. On Twitter, you want to start following everything and anything Dodgers related to spread your lie. Brooklyn Dodgers, Los Angeles Dodgers, Vin Scully, you name it, if it is Dodgers related, you follow it. But here's one thing you don't do: Don't sit on Twitter Search and follow or talk to random people who happen to be talking about the Dodgers. That's just spamming, and you want to position yourself as an "expert," not a spammer. Start tweeting with the people related to "your field" (you can find them from their Web sites and with some googling). Don't pitch them anything yet. Just show up on their Web sites, leave comments, retweet what they're saying, and pretend to care about what they're talking about.

Wait. "Pretend" to care. Aren't you "engaging" and "building relationships" with the "community?" Fuck that crap! You're furthering your own agenda. All this other shit is just how marketers make this stuff look positive, when in fact they're trying to line their own pockets. Remember, the whole point here is to get these suckers to notice you, and in doing so, bring them to your Web site. If you do everything I laid out for you, they will. Oh, one more thing: If you have the money, hire "sock puppets"—people who can post blog comments, message board comments, Facebook posts, and comments on community news Web sites that casually mention you or your blog. Don't overdo it—they shouldn't write more than one post about you for every eight or so about other things. The trick is to not be obvious. You're gaming people, but I'm going to assume, given that you're spreading a lie about yourself, that you're totally fine with crossing some ethical lines. And these "sock puppets" work, that's why the rich and corporations pay millions of dollars to use them to clean up their search results and to steer online discussions toward a more favorable outcome. If we, as humans, see other people saying positive and nice things, we're more likely to be swayed, especially if we don't know that person saying those nice things is being paid to do so.

## Putting the "Long" in "Long Con"

STEP 4: After about a year of seeding the Web (anything less and people will think you're gaming them, which you are, but you don't want them to know that), if any of those blogs allow for people to do guest posts, get yourself the opportunity to write one. If you're on a message board (yes, they still exist, they never left), you can then post about stuff related to your field of "expertise." Waiting is key; if you don't wait, it will result in your banning and being labeled as a spammer in the community. If the reporters you're following bring up anything even remotely related to your area of "expertise"—in our case, the return of the Brooklyn Dodgers, or a baseball team like the Oakland A's looking to move—contact them, show them your Web site, play up the benefits of what you have to offer, and see if they'll cover the story.

But never, ever, say "Is this something you might be interested in writing about?" You can bet the answer will be no. Instead just give them the "facts," and if you continue to maintain and update your Web site, they'll link to it or reference it in future posts.

Don't stop at specialized blogs, either. It isn't hard to contribute bullshit to a site like The Huffington Post, as you've seen. They won't pay you, but that's fine in this scenario because the only real benefit they can offer anyone is that Google likes stuff posted there. So a post about why the Dodgers should come back, for instance, is very likely to appear for any related searches. The Huffington Post may arguably be exploiting writers, but as long as Google allows the site to manipulate them, there's no reason why you can't exploit Google in the same way.

Then go to places like Mashable and other tech blogs, where they often allow CEOs and employees of companies whom they cover to write posts playing up their industry, and find a way to tie in what you do with their topic. No blog is too small to contribute to, so post your bullshit everywhere!

(There's a reason I call it "The Long Con of the Experts." It takes a *really* long time to build up enough traffic and credibility in the eyes of the people you need, to advance to the next step, especially when you're doing this without any money. All you can do is update your blog, stalk people on Twitter (the right way), leave comments everywhere, do guest posts, keep using the keywords you settled on, and continue your "research." As long as no one figures out what your end goal is, you'll be fine.)

But as I mentioned earlier: the Web can only take you so far. After a while, you've expanded as far as you can. If you're beating the same drum you were a year later without a book deal or consulting gigs to speak of, people are going to get sick of you and your story. Your "expertise" is going to start to look a bit questionable. So you need the media to get behind you in a bigger way.

**Step 5:** Here let's imagine the Brooklyn Dodgers myth that I've been selling—that it's inevitable, that I'm an expert, that I can help you be prepared—is picked up by a few mid-size media outlets. (In chapter 17, I'll show you how to do this.) Once one media outlet quotes you, you're in, and others will be more likely to do the same. The media's massive failure to look critically at this sort of thing is a key component of the Asshole-Based Economy. If the media had done any fact checking, they would know that you were a pretender. They would also know that "social media" wasn't much more than a clever ruse. Tron Guy (that's right . . . Internet sensation Tron Guy) told me, "Put simply, the Internet, collectively, is the greatest bullshit detector ever invented."[5] That might be true, but like any good lie detector, it also has some serious flaws. In this case, what you see on the Internet is heavily determined by what the traditional media is talking about. The media, and people taking what "experts" say for granted, is one of those flaws. The key point right now is that it's not likely someone in the press will call bullshit on your "expertise." That will only come later after you start making a lot of money. If the media is including you in this coverage, they think you're legit, and given enough time (and potentially connecting with the right people), you should be able to crack into the larger media markets.

For me, that would be New York. When it comes to baseball nostalgia, you'd be hard-pressed to find a better hook than what bringing the Dodgers back to Brooklyn would mean for the city and for baseball. Trust me. No one is going to miss the Mets.

**Step 6:** If you know how to get attention for yourself, and appear to have an audience (whether or not you actually have one doesn't matter), this makes you attractive to agents and publishers. If *you* look like you can sell books, and have the *appearance* of knowing what you're talking about, publishers will want to work with you. The illusion that you're running with something that already has an audience makes you attractive to any company in the entertainment business. Not just book publishers.

And once you're in with that book deal, you're able to start positioning yourself as a speaker and consultant on the subject. All you need to do is add a mention of your forthcoming book on your Web site, start sending short pitch e-mails. If you've positioned yourself as an expert in relocating baseball teams, and if you play your cards right, given enough media attention and any potential traction on the Web, the teams will start coming to you. This is especially true with minor league sports as most teams tend to move frequently.

**STEP 7:** Let's say you sell your book, it comes out, and you get even more media coverage. Again, nothing you're selling is truthful or accurate. The imminent arrival of the Brooklyn Dodgers that I've been selling—and the notion that I'm an expert—are a fiction (sad as it is to say). In the case of "social media," the fiction is that these platforms are something new, or that you've got something new and fresh to say about them. But, thanks to that book, the larger media outlets will now give you credibility, and that means speaking agencies will work to book you, at a tidy sum per engagement, to spout your bullshit.

So now you're traveling around the country—maybe the world—spreading your message, and people are buying it because the media has vouched for you as an "Expert." And thanks to the nature of the Asshole-Based Economy, audiences around the world are going to be buying it precisely because of all the newfound attention.

If your book doesn't sell? Perhaps because you don't have a Hollywood agent to get you on television, or thousands of dollars to pay for a publicist, or the media just gets sick of your story, your time in the club will expire. That's good for us, who are spared your fictions—but it's not a good thing for you. You need these traditional outlets to continue covering you so you can up your speaking fees.

So, what do you do when the well dries up? Easy: You dig a new one. As I showed you, the marketers do this all the time. Right now the "social media" well is drying up, so they are starting to move on—to "gamification," "big data," or "the mobile Web." What they sell has to change because none of it has a long shelf-life. Search engine optimization (SEO) had a good seven years in the spotlight, but then it gave way to blogging. Then blogging gave way to "social media," which is now giving way to the next generation. (And don't sweat this "mobile Web" thing. Eventually there will be one standard way for all your devices to display everything on the Web in one set way. That may be HTML5, it may be something else. So, although we're not quite there yet, there will be virtually no difference between "the Web" and "the mobile Web."

Bullshit is *always* evolving, which is why it's so important when you're first starting out to explore multiple angles of the subject you are researching. The Brooklyn Dodgers returning to Brooklyn myth may get you a book deal and maybe the attention of other teams if you play up your expertise on team relocation. But you need to hold the audience's attention, which means producing more bullshit. And the odds are the second you start getting attention for yourself, other people of dubious distinction will start to mimic what you're doing. That's exactly what happened with "social media." Coupled with the timing of the Great Recession and the amount of media attention Gary Vaynerchuk got as a "social media success story," people from other fields who were left unemployed took up "social media" marketing as a profession. If these amateur marketers see you getting attention for creating bullshit, you can bet they're going to start selling it, too, and the worst part is that they'll probably just regurgitate what you're saying. If you asked me to identify a Voldemort in the myth of "social media," it would be these people, and not guys like Gary Vaynerchuk. Ultimately, Gary has clients he has to answer to, but these amateur marketers don't, meaning they can bleed one business dry after another. Each time they get fired, they move right on to the next victim without conscience.

If all has gone well in spreading your own lies, you should have an audience. With your credibility, visibility, and the support of the media, you can say pretty much whatever you want. And with the evolution of "Digital Reputation Management," with help from those sock puppets, for example, you can totally stifle any critical posts that may surface on Google and other places. Meaning, your myth can continue to grow unchecked long after you've moved on to a new subject, much in the same way amateur marketers can bury anything bad said about them long enough to move on to a new client.

And if someone *does* call you out on your bullshit claims? Do what the Cyber Hipsters do: Bury the bad information. The good news is that even though Digital Reputation Management firms are expensive, their techniques are easy to copy (for now, until Google catches on). Here is what those experts do:

1. Use sock puppets to appear in comments sections on blogs, on message boards, and on social networks wherever something negative is said. The sock puppet should defend that person and provide a link to something favorable about them (and be sure to look like a convincing "real person," as I described above). Scott Adams, creator of the popular Dilbert comic strips, was caught doing this on Reddit, responding to negative comments about himself and Dilbert under the pseudonym "PlannedChaos."[6]
2. Have your sock puppet enter favorable terms into Google about the person they're defending at least once a day, and have them place on Web sites links to the person you're defending's Web site using fa-

vorable key words as part of that link. This used to be known as a Google Bomb, and although Google made changes to their algorithm, the strategy for creating one hasn't changed. (Try googling "Santorum" some time.) The most famous Google Bomb was the time when George Johnson, a Washington computer programmer, embarked on a campaign to make the home page for then President George W. Bush be the top search result in Google when you entered "miserable failure."[7] Although it's harder to execute a Google Bomb today, it's still easy to manipulate and hide things on Google, and Google's failure to act has allowed similar tactics like this to remain effective.

3. Hire someone that has Wikipedia editorial credentials to edit any problematic Wikipedia pages. And while you're at it, hire someone to submit links that positively portray you and your scam to Digg, Reddit, Twitter, and Facebook. This is a common practice that reaches all the way to the top users on all of these Web sites. Although he told me he has never been paid to submit something directly, Andrew Sorcini (better known on Digg and other networks as "Mr. Baby Man") said, "Because of my experience at recognizing viral content, I've been quite successful at helping companies craft original content that is intended to organically appeal to users of social media sites such as Digg, Reddit, Facebook, and Twitter [ . . . ] Because of existing NDAs, I'm not allowed to name names, but one task I've had was to cull through thousands of archival local news articles from several major news outlets and find ways to repurpose that content so it would appeal on a national scale to current audiences. Also remember 'Sharktopus' frenzy? I may or may not have had something to do with that."

4. And finally, sock puppets should create their own content about you on places like Blogger, which unlike Tumblr, is easily found in Google's search results to help push down anything bad.

Scary, huh? But no less effective. You now have a fail-proof way of spreading bullshit and getting paid in the process

But this is as scary as it is infuriating. Trying to sell something and make money off what you love doing? It's virtually impossible without the right (old-fashioned) connections, a lot of luck, the support of the media, and any number of factors that are usually beyond your control. But if you want to make that bullshit up, package it, and sell it, the Web makes it fairly easy to do. The great bullshit detector, as it turns out, is the biggest and best method to spread and profit from bullshit that was ever invented.

This, in a nutshell, is why there are so many "social media" marketers selling stuff that doesn't work. It's easy, and barring intervention by the FTC[8], improved consumer awareness about the scam (the goal of this book, if you haven't already gathered), and Google reconsidering a system that currently rewards the churning out of a million posts a day, regardless of their value, and the easy burial of the truth, the myths will keep on coming.

# PART IV

# HOW TO *REALLY* MAKE IT ON THE WEB

---

"It is common sense to take a method and try it: If it fails, admit
it frankly and try another. But above all, try something."
—*President Franklin Delano Roosevelt, former president and
American badass*

## CHAPTER SEVENTEEN

# EVERYTHING YOU WILL EVER NEED TO KNOW ABOUT MARKETING

———————

**THIS BOOK HAS BEEN BROKEN** up into four parts. First, I told you why "social media" is bullshit. In the second part, I told you how that bullshit came to prominence (and who was responsible for that). In the previous section, I showed you how bullshit spreads on the Internet, so now you should be able to spot it in the wild and put a stop to it.

And now, we've come to the end. This is where I tell you what I know about marketing, drawn from online marketing successes and failures too countless and humiliating to mention.

I'm not out to make a fortune in telling you this. Believe me, anyone (besides the marketers, who are just using the book as an oversized business card) who tells you they wrote a book to make money, especially in this economy, is either crazy or a liar. This time next year, I'll probably still be living in a studio apartment somewhere.

This book is meant to help. I don't do consulting. I don't do workshops. I don't invest in any of the companies I talk about. I don't even have a desire to do public speaking unless there are bricks behind me and I'm getting heckled by a guy with a mullet. What I am looking to do is tell the truth. That's why this book exists in the first place. I could have easily just stuck with writing *Dracula and Kittens*[1] and making people laugh, but the truth was too important. I don't like to see good people get screwed, and that's what's happening. I hope in bringing the truth to you, you will stand up with me and spread the word. America is perceived as an every-man-and-woman-for-themselves kind of place, but it's not. It's a place where we look out for each other and take care of our own. And part of doing that is calling out bullshit like "social media." That brings us to the last part of this book: the advice.

The old-fashioned marketing advice—the stuff that authors have been writing about for decades—*does* work. It's the other stuff, the stuff used to fill out books and keynote addresses—that's the problem.

The reason the generic stuff works is because it has all been done, proven, and tested since Jesus rode around on a Brontasaurus. On my desk right now is a second edition of *How to Win Friends and Influence People*. After reading almost every popular marketing book that's come out since 2001, and this book, originally published in 1936, I can conclude one thing: If Dale Carnegie were alive today, he'd sue all these guys for plagiarism. (And if Jesus were alive today, he'd sue Carnegie for doing the same.) Almost every marketing book that has come out since *How to Win Friends and Influence People* is just putting a new spin on what Carnegie talked about seventy-five years ago. So it shouldn't come as a surprise then to see, for example, "social media" expert and author Erik Qualman refer to himself as "The Digital Dale Carnegie" on his Web site.[2]

If you want to challenge my assessment, I encourage you to go to the library, take out a copy of *How to Win Friends and Influence People*, and then read a marketing book released this year. If it doesn't blow your mind, it'll at least make you regret wasting so much money on marketing books. (I'm well into the thousands on that front; I feel your pain.) So, let's get the generic, but useful, marketing advice out of the way once and for all!

TIP #1: As FDR, the perennial number three on most lists of the greatest American presidents, once said, "It is common sense to take a method and try it: If it fails, admit it frankly and try another. But above all, try something."[3] So put the work in and stick with what you're doing when no one is reading, buying, or following anything that you do. Telling people to have "passion" is redundant. I assume that if you're doing something with your own time and money, you're passionate about it. So it's not about passion, it's about being happy. If what you do makes you happy, that's all that matters. Even if you fail. The way I see it? You could be dead tomorrow, so you might as well enjoy what you're doing.

## Meet The Press

TIP #2: Except in rare cases, you won't be able to get anywhere in marketing anything without the press. The good news is that you can do almost all of the press yourself. All you have to do is take what you do and make it into a story people will be interested in—especially your grandmother. If *she* gets it, so will everyone else. The more the story is tied into the geographic area of the media outlet you're targeting, the better. The best way to think about it is like this: If you live in New York City, you think the world ends at the Holland Tunnel. Granted, the Holland Tunnel empties out into New Jersey, so that's mostly true. But if you live in New York City, you're not overly concerned about what happens in Jersey City. It's like this all across America. Unless it's tied into where people live and work, barring a threat to their safety or well-being, they don't care. Even if it's happening in another city ten minutes away. (Just ask the people in Dallas how they feel about the people in Forth Worth sometime. There's a reason the Texas Rangers play in Arlington and not either of those two cities.)

So how do you deal with that? You can start by working with someone from each area you want to target. For example, working with a local business will give you an "anchor" that many local and regional media outlets look for. Without that anchor, you won't be able to get coverage from them.

You also need to develop "hooks." The more exciting you can make what you're pitching, the better. It's easy to poke fun at the "Hollywood shorthand," but it works. If I came to you and said I wanted to pitch a movie called "Charlie Thunder," and you asked me what it was, I'd tell you "It's *Welcome Back, Kotter* meets *The Wrestler*." (You laugh now—wait until you see it in theaters.) The Hollywood shorthand creates a quick, easy idea that people will get intuitively when you pitch it to them, and it'll make your pitch that much easier for them to sell to their editors. Not to mention, the Hollywood shorthand is a great way to amuse yourself when you're bored. Go ahead and think about what *The Golden Girls* meets *Man Tracker* would look like as a show.

Now, you don't want to use the Hollywood shorthand just for news stories, but also in the way you conceive of your business. Keeping it easy to understand and, hopefully, exciting in some way. As Evan White, chief marketing officer at Viddy, Inc. put it, "Journalists need a hook that will resonate with their readers or viewers. This hook is different for every journalist, and every news outlet. But what doesn't change is the fact that they need one. This hook could be anything from a seemingly unreachable goal like trading a red paperclip for a house or hitchhiking to fifty state capitols in fifty days (both happened). Or it can be plain facts, like [that] six cute, furry gray puppies are actually the most-watched video in the history of videos, with millions of hours logged every day. The bottom line is a journalist needs something that sounds exciting enough to get approval from their editor on."[4]

But having an anchor and a hook doesn't necessarily help with the national outlets or bigger cities. With them you want to find the most appropriate reporter to get in touch with. You can determine this by going through that media outlet's archives and seeing what that reporter tends to cover. (And don't ever send anything to a bulk e-mail address that looks like news@mediaoutlet.com. No one will read it.) If you can't find a specific reporter's email address, call the media outlet and ask for it. The Web and all of these platforms have made the phone and snail mail *more* effective to use, not less. If everyone is using one platform, that means there might be an opportunity to get in using one they don't.

Once you have that e-mail, put a short pitch together (no more than a paragraph) and send it to the reporter. If they ask for more info, then send them a press release. If you don't know how to write a press release, google it. There are plenty of "How To's" and templates you can borrow from. (Just make sure you don't quote yourself in your own press release. That just makes you sound like an asshole. Have other people, like your local anchor, quoted instead.) And if possible, make sure if there is an online version of the story, it links to your Web site. Google's algorithms love in-bound links from the media, and although that algorithm changes often, it's always going to be based on the popularity and credibility of sites linking to you, that's the foundation upon which Google was founded. And when it comes to in-bound links, you're not going to find a better place to get them than the media.

If the local media picks up the story and the regional outlet in your area doesn't contact you to do their own, rinse and repeat the process of pitching with the regional outlet. Most of the time, media coverage breeds media coverage, but sometimes you'll have to take that extra step. And then you just keep doing this all the way to the national level. As Evan added, "I always say that press breeds press. And it's not just local to regional to national. I think radio leads to print, and radio is usually pretty easy to get. Think about it; anchors get sixty minutes, editors get a few pages, but radio hosts fill hours of air time. I once called a radio station in Branson, Missouri, and literally five minutes later my client was on the air."

When it comes to the nationals and large cities like New York, Washington, D.C., and Los Angeles, be prepared to get ignored. Try contacting them on your own anyway, and if you're not getting enough traction, hire a publicist. Just because those outlets will ignore it, doesn't mean you shouldn't try to reach them. Evan says, "When you're talking about the largest media markets . . . you need something with mass appeal. These markets syndicate to nearly all of the smaller markets, so the story needs to be something that everyone can easily connect with."[5]

As for television, in addition to a local anchor, there needs to be a visual component to the story. I contributed to the Wounded Warriors Family Support High Five Tour, working for Colonel John Folsom, which involved the colonel driving a car across the country and soliciting donations. The colonel chose a Shelby Mustang wrapped in the red, white, and blue. I suggested that he consider something more environmentally friendly, to which he gently replied that people who drive environmentally friendly cars are pussies.[6] As it turns out, the colonel was a marketing genius. The red-white-and-blue-wrapped mustang is a killer visual. He also came up with the idea of having people sign the vehicle at each stop, which adds a bit of drama that the media, particularly television, loved. Why are those people signing the mustang? Why is the colonel high-fiving people? All of those things are highly visual. So if you're going to try to get the attention of the television media, you have to figure out what that visual component is going to be.

I'll let Jacquie Jordan, former television producer and author of *Get on TV!*, get the last word in on this subject. According to Jacquie, the best way to get television interviews is to "make sure to only focus on the producers who create content. When in doubt over some obscure producing prefix, keep this simple rule in mind: always aim for content producers . . . You should target your pitch [to]: researchers, bookers, associate producers, segment producers, and producers. They are the core group that are working the phone and searching the Web. They are the people reading the newspaper articles and ripping out headlines for their shows. They choose every element that goes into . . . the show itself."[7]

A brief word about publicists: Before you hire one, make sure to interview many candidates; get references and case studies; and ask "Who can you connect me to?" If they can't plug you into a national outlet, don't hire them. And don't ever hire anyone to do anything you can do yourself. That's why so many publicists and other service providers get a bad rap. A bad rap could put you in the hospital. People usually hire these people for the wrong reason, without properly evaluating them, and then get mad when they produce results they don't like. Do everything you can yourself first, using the Internet to learn about the stuff you don't know how to do. Once you've exhausted those options, or find that you don't have the time, then you can hire someone to work with you.

Always do your homework. Plenty of people *don't*, and that's why so many of these marketers are able to sneak in their bullshit. If you question them on it, you'll see pretty fast who is full of it, and who isn't. And as you saw in this book, the wheels on the "social media" bus come off fast when you start to take a good look at it, but you have to know what to look for, too. What kind of questions should you ask? Write down what your situation is, what your budget is, what your goals are, and then work backward from there. Be as specific as possible because everyone's needs and situation are different. Someone who might be the "expert" on one thing might not be the expert that's right for you.

PR drives everything. It was that way when the hoax of the Cardiff

Giant made national headlines in the 1860s, and it's been a staple of our society since PR was made into a profession in the early 1920s. If you were to take any book that gives advice on press and publicity, you'll find that nearly all—like today's marketing books do for *How to Win Friends and Influence People*—recycle Edward Bernays's *Crystallizing Public Opinion*. The only difference? They use way more buzzwords. (*Crystallizing Public Opinion*, by the way, came out in 1923.)[8]

Most PR people get paid a retainer regardless of whether or not they accomplish anything for you. This is also true for many advertising agencies hired by large corporations. So there's no direct incentive for them to succeed—apart from, of course, your continued business. Always shop around, and if it comes down to a PR person who gets paid based on results as opposed to a general retainer, all other things being equal, hire the person who gets paid based on results.[9][10]

## Playing in the Big Leagues

**TIP #3.** Throughout the book you've heard me mention "the majors." Let's think about what that means for a second.

But first, a word about content: If what you have sucks, then it's not going to go anywhere, no matter what you do and where you put it. That much of what Gary Vanderchuk said back in chapter 4 is true. That's also why so much stuff on the Web doesn't go anywhere: Almost all of it sucks. That's not an attack on amateur content. Frankly, it's hard to make a distinction between amateur and professional content anymore, and determining quality is a subjective thing. So I won't bother. Here I'm referring to *all* of it. And what's not subjective is that if something is done well, regardless of who made it, it will get shared . . . to a point.

Trying to advance yourself using the platforms I've discussed in this book is a lot like playing at a Vegas casino. The "game" the marketers always talk about is against you from the start. It's rigged in such a way that if you're trying to move forward as a small business, artist, or entrepreneur who makes something of value, it's virtually impossible to win. And the concept of "making something"—as opposed to selling your commentary—is important to distinguish here. Jeff Jarvis, Clay Shirky, Jay Rosen, Brian Solis, Chris Brogan, the people at Mashable, the Altimeter Group—many of the people I told you about in this book don't *make* anything. They comment. They talk. They bullshit. They're not concerned with the day-to-day operations of your business, or getting your band to sell out Madison Square Garden, or helping your start-up change the world. This isn't to say that what these guys produce isn't without value, but what they've done is exploit an opportunity to get attention, and a fair amount of wealth, without much of a product. Something that's infuriatingly easy to do.

So, how does "the game" really work?

Imagine you're playing for the online equivalent of the Great Lakes Loons, the Single-A baseball affiliate of the Los Angeles Dodgers based in Midland, Michigan. You're there because you have a dream of playing in the majors. Everyone who follows the same basic, generic marketing advice can, with enough perseverance and luck, make it to the equivalent of, say, the Chattanooga Lookouts, the Double-A club. At that point, they start to hit dead ends. Either people lose interest in pushing their product, their product isn't really great enough to elevate beyond that level, or they have a good idea but the wrong audience. (The list goes on, but based on my experience, it's almost always that last one. Josh Kaufman, author of the excellent *The Personal MBA*, referred to this as the "Iron Law of the Market"—"If people don't want what you provide or what you create, you're screwed.")[11]

If you walk away from this book only remembering one thing, let it be that: It's not about "the community." It's about *your customer*. If you've got your customers wrong, nothing you do is going to matter. For small businesses, artists, and entrepreneurs, the only metric that matters are sales. The customer is *not* always right (and we'll get to what to do when they bad-mouth you later). But if you don't know who they are, you're not going anywhere. Who those customers are determines price, location, platform, and media for reaching them—you name it. So ask questions, conduct surveys, look at who is visiting your Web site, how long they're staying there and what they're clicking on. That information is way more valuable than how many visitors and page views you have.[12] Get as much information as you can and start to work with what you collect. And if you're lost, remember: Don't hire anyone until you've exhausted all your options first because you'll do a better job than they will on most things. Instead try free sources of advice for small-business owners like those at SCORE (Score.org) and the U.S. Small Business Administration (SBA.gov).

The people who survive the AA-affiliate cuts by addressing these problems have a shot at moving up to the Albuquerque Isotopes, the Dodgers' Triple-A team. Unfortunately, nothing any marketing author tells you can get you beyond that. You may never play for the Dodgers. As I mentioned earlier, there's a lot to be said for luck, timing, and the millions of other specific factors that play into any business's success. As far as luck and timing go, the best thing you can do is be prepared. If you are, and an opportunity presents itself, you'll be ready for it.

The good news is that you can make a comfortable living at the Triple-A level. And maybe that's as far as you want to go. You're going to have way more freedom to produce what you want on this level than you will at the majors, because the machinery of the majors isn't set up to support things like creative freedom. As Adam Carolla told me, "There's no way I'd be able to do what I do with my podcast on Comedy Central. The second it got on there, they'd put it in front of a live audience. Then add a warm-up comic, and then send me notes telling me to shorten things up. It's far easier and less expensive for them to tape a stand-up and air that or take clips off YouTube and make fun of them. I like the autonomy that comes with doing the podcast, and there's no place on television where you can do what I'm doing."[13] That's why you have hundreds of cable channels with almost all running some variation of another channel's popular show. Media companies do this because that other channel's show is popular, and popular shows mean more advertising dollars. Shows that are creative and well produced but don't pull in a huge audience get cancelled because they don't pull in big enough numbers to justify the cost of producing them.[14]

The decision makers at the major league level are being a lot like the pilot from the short story "The Cold Equations" by Tom Godwin. At the climax of the story, a stowaway is jettisoned into space because the ship she's carried on only has enough fuel to carry its intended cargo. The girl is dead weight, and her continued presence on the ship endangers the mission. So, the pilot has no choice. The corporations that make all the decisions at the major league level are a lot like that pilot. The ship they're running is designed a certain way; if it doesn't make money, they have to fix it. And since we're talking hundreds of millions of dollars here, these companies need to produce products that have the broadest possible appeal. This also makes them risk averse, which makes it harder for new players to get called up and have a chance to swing the bat.

On the major league level, there are also corporate and special interests that exert an influence on you, and which would otherwise ignore you at the Triple-A level. If you produce something your sponsor doesn't like, they can pull the funding and kill your project. Comcast pulled an $18,000 grant to the not-for-profit Reel Grrls organization in 2011 over a tweet from the group knocking Comcast's should-have-been-illegal hiring of former FCC commissioner Meredith Baker. Comcast later reversed their decision on pulling the grant, but only after *The Washington Post* and other media outlets picked up the story.[15]

One of the goals of this book is to show you the environment you're actually trying to succeed in, not the idealized version many marketers want to show you, and by doing so, I hope you'll figure out a way to advance to the majors on your own (or choose not to advance to the majors, if you prefer).

## The Golden Rule of the Internet

TIP #4. Don't be a dick.

## The *Real* Golden Rule of the Internet

TIP #5. If you're considering using the social networks and publishing tools on the Web to create something you can't elsewhere; and if you know your audience uses the platforms; and if you have the time to invest in really working with them; and you're confident that your efforts can produce measurable results for you; then yes, use them. But remember: Not using them won't harm you in *any way*. The idea that you're "leaving money on the table" by not using them is patently false.[16] Unless you're Miss Cleo, there's no way to know what the outcome of your decisions will be. Yet marketers, Cyber Hipsters, analysts, and their friends use this sort of thinking to prey on you, small businesses, artists, and entreprenuers.

Personally? I like Twitter. Of the Big Six "social media" platforms, it's the only one I feel comfortable suggesting, for reasons I mentioned in previous chapters. But even Twitter I only recommend in limited circumstances. If your business is in New York City? You should probably have a Twitter account. The reason for this is simple: Twitter's creator, Jack Dorsey, said that New York has the most Twitter users in the world.[17] You don't need it, of course. But I'm convinced that in this specific case, it won't hurt. Other cities are a different story. In fact, I can safely say that if you don't live in a major city like Los Angeles, Chicago, New York, Austin, or San Francisco, you can safely skip out on Twitter. (By the way, if your audience is over fifty? Ditto.)

New York City is a bit of an extreme. In a market that big, especially one where it's impossible to get local coverage without a killer hook, you should explore all of the options available to you.

But, most of us *don't* live in those cities, so it doesn't matter. And that's an important point to remember: Most of the people who write these marketing books come out of places like New York, Los Angeles, San Francisco, and a handful of other major metropolitan areas. Media coverage is everything because it in turn fuels what winds up on these platforms, and in most places, it's way easier to get than it is in a place like New York. Yet the marketers all write as if what's true for them is true for everyone. It's not.

Does having a presence on these platforms hurt you? No. It doesn't hurt to have a social networking profile or presence on a publishing platform like Twitter. But there has to be a point behind having one. Being on Facebook for the sake of being on Facebook is stupid. I use Twitter because I like to write jokes, and it forces me to be a better writer due to the limit on characters in a message. But you shouldn't be there just because everyone else is or because some marketer told you to be there. Social networks and publishing platforms shouldn't be a time or resource drain for you. At best, they should be an added bonus.

If you do use these services, make sure you're putting some effort into it, and that your audience is there in the first place. A half-assed presence on these things is way, way worse than not having any at all. So be prepared to invest a lot of time and energy if you do. Remember: People will make your product or service known on there for you as long as you make it easy for them to do so. You, as an individual, can have an account to make connections or even just for fun, but your product or business doesn't need one. Make it easy to share, and then exhaust all your offline alternatives first—in terms of media exposure, networking, advertising—before doing anything online.

Then, and only then, should you make the jump. The decision rests with you, not the marketers, Cyber Hipsters, and their friends.

## If They're Talking About You Behind Your Back, They're Talking to Your Ass

**TIP #6.** A high school teacher once said that to me, and since the Internet and its platforms are pretty much just high school on steroids, this is as true today as it was then. Especially given the 1 percent Rule, which says that when it comes to Internet comments, it's small, vocal minority doing the talk—not anyone else. The only time those comments become a "social media crisis," as the Altimeter Group might spin them, is when the real media gets involved. Nobody else cares what's being said about you on Yelp or on YouTube.

There are some more extreme cases involving websites like Reddit, Digg, and 4Chan, involving the formation of an "Internet lynch mob." When those occur, and you're not at fault, there's really not much you can do but ride it out and not feed it any further. And those are specific to just these few sites because they have the ability to perpetuate themselves—until the mob cools. These days, now that Digg is mostly irrelevant and Reddit is being heavily policed by its corporate owner, these sorts of things will become increasingly rare. When the mob forms on the other "social media" platforms, they usually fade without the media's intervention, especially if you stay out of it. (Apart from an apology and a correction to the problem, if you were at fault.)

So, what about customer service? If someone is bashing you on the

Web or on a social network, shouldn't you have a profile to counter them? No. Most people won't see the comment, and in a place like Yelp, your good customers will come to your rescue if you encourage them to do so. (If you get involved you could come off like Scott Adams did when he was defending himself on Metafilter under a pseudonym. Even if Adams was right about something, he still came off like a dick. I also once made this mistake with the *Chicago Reader*.[18] They were having some fun at the expense of something I posted on The Huffington Post. I responded like a dick and came out worse for wear. Not to mention: If you say something stupid on someone else's Web site, unless they're cool about it, that comment could live forever. My dumb comments are still on that particular *Chicago Reader* post, despite asking them to take it down multiple times over the years. Lesson learned: Fighting with people on the Internet is a lot like being in a car accident; nobody comes out looking good.

The best customer service is offered in person, over the phone, and if those other options are exhausted, by e-mail. The phone is your best weapon. Take your phone number and list it prominently everywhere that you ultimately invest your time, money, and resources into. The people with legitimate customer concerns will contact you using any of the three methods, but listing your phone number and actively managing your calls in a friendly, reasonable way tells customers you're serious about resolving their problems. If you have a problem with this book, or just want to talk about it, you can call me at 518-832-9844. If I don't pick up, leave a message for me and I *will* call you back.[19]

As far as venues like Yelp or Amazon, there's no reason to fight negativity on their turf. If you're worried about their comments showing up in search engine results for your business, then produce good, original content (videos, pictures, blog posts) on a regular basis on your Web site and through your friends' and partners' Web sites. Maintain a database of customers (a mailing list) who identify themselves as satisfied, and ask them to provide their honest feedback about you on these Web sites and services. If you feel like that still isn't enough, then you can create a profile for your business or project on prominent social networks and publishing tools and produce original, good content there, too. It's not necessary, nor do I recommend you use any of these platforms except Twitter (sometimes), but if it'll give you peace of mind, do it. All of this content creation will flush the bad results out of Google, and if your customers have got your back, you won't have to worry about what strangers on Yelp say about you.

## Mel Brooks Was Right: "Tweaking. Always Tweaking"

TIP #7. On November 7, 2007, Mel Brooks was interviewed on the *NBC Evening News* by Brian Williams about the premier of *Young Frankenstein* on Broadway. He was asked, essentially, what kept him busy, and his response was "Tweaking. Always tweaking. Change a line, change a tune. Always. Tweaking."[20]

That always stuck with me. You should always be tweaking. Look for opportunities to tweak and improve everything that you do. Brooks was making changes to the *Young Frankenstein* musical until, and after, opening night. If he could find a way to make the show better by tweaking it, he would. It's easy to say "Make a great product, make sure it's easy to use and understand, network, work the press, and you'll be successful." That's pretty much where every marketing book's good advice ends. But few talk about the importance of testing your idea before taking it public. Although there are obstacles in place that keep you from getting to the majors, there's no reason to be unprepared for the possibility of getting there. You should be prepared for everything, no matter how unlikely. You just don't know what the future holds, and the only way to be prepared is to continue to improve what you're doing.

That doesn't mean freak out when some random person gives you advice on Facebook, or a poor review on Yelp. It just means be mindful of all the advice you get, actively seek it out, and if you see a pattern emerge, investigate whether or not you should make a change.

There is no better book available on the importance of testing your Web efforts (and how to do it inexpensively) than *Don't Make Me Think!* by Steve Krug. If you don't own that book, *buy it*. As far as testing your product or idea goes, see what your friends think, see what their friends think, and try it out locally first. You only get one good shot when introducing a product to a national audience, so you want to work out the kinks on the local and regional level as much as possible. Your friends, your community, and your city are great places to start collecting feedback and making adjustments. The more flaws you work out, the less risky your product or idea looks to the people making the decisions in the majors.

## CHAPTER EIGHTEEN
# RECAP

———————

**THIS CHAPTER IS** meant to serve as an "Executive Summary" for *Social Media Is Bullshit*. It's a recap of the different items and themes mentioned throughout the book. You know, in the event you've been multitasking while reading this and don't remember a damn thing I've said, this section is also for idiots like me who keep buying books despite the fact they've got twelve of them to read and no time to actually read them.

### EVERYTHING YOU NEED TO KNOW FROM
### *SOCIAL MEDIA IS BULLSHIT*

* Offline matters more than online. *This will never change.* Your location, your circumstances, your audience, that determines *everything*. Trying to make a million dollars off a niche platform on the Web is a bad idea. Not many people can do it, and most of those who do are either trying to sell you something, were in the

right place at the right time, had the right connections, or get backing from the media in some form. I'm not saying you can't, but I'm saying there's a better way to survive and thrive by doing something that makes you happy. It's just a lot slower and way less glamorous.

+ The Long Tail is bullshit. It just doesn't work, and it's a bad business model if you're not a media outlet. You can target niche audiences. That part is true. But that niche must have enough of a critical mass behind it to support your business. Most don't. There's also no reason why you can't target as broad an audience as possible.

+ Ninety-nine percent of the things that are often referred to as "viral" are driven by offline forces: real-world connections, traditional media, legitamate celebrities, corporate spending. For the small fraction that remains, it has a lot to do with being in the right place at the right time, using the right keywords at the right moment, or having one of the big corporate blogs latch onto something that's popular with a smaller community Web site, so they can squeeze page views out of it. But in the end, making something "go viral" in the organic way is the product of guess work, and it's incredibly unlikely that something you do will go "viral." The odds are better that you'll be struck by lightning.

+ The concept that if you put something online "people will see it" is not true. Most YouTube videos go unwatched and most Web sites go unvisited.

+ Momentum is everything on the Web. You can have the funniest content in the world, or the coolest product, but unless there's momentum behind it, nothing you do is going to matter. It's not going to spread just by virtue of your putting it out there. Momentum is built by using the connections you've established—the old-fashioned way—to help get the word out, and then sustained by going to the press and doing further outreach. Once it looks like you have some momentum (you'll know because you'll start getting more e-mail), then everything else will kick in: People will share your stuff on the various networks, *on their own*, because they want to and they see other people doing the same.

- Be skeptical of metrics like "awareness" and "engagement." These and other "social media" metrics don't really mean anything. People who talk about them make big promises of what these metrics can deliver, but there's *no proof* that they ever have in a meaningful way that can be easily replicated—unlike with television where they immediately close hit shows and reap high ratings. Even the large corporations who are often touted as having had "social media success stories" don't see "social media" as a money-maker. They see it as a loss leader. The rest of us can't afford to be in that position. The only metric that matters for small businesses, artists, and entrepreneurs is sales. If you're not making money, you can't keep doing what you're doing. It's as simple as that. (And as far as the Web goes, the only metric that matters is unique visitors *coupled with* how much time they spend with you and what they click on. The number of unique visitors on its own, like page views, users, free app downloads, followers, fans, likes, and YouTube views, is meaningless.)

- Question everything. When it comes to hiring someone to work for you—which, again, you shouldn't do until you've exhausted all your *free* alternatives and have tried to do as much as you can yourself—ask them a lot of questions. You'll be able to spot someone who is trying to sell you bullshit from someone who actually knows what they're doing if they can give you actual facts and figures, not to mention testimonials, case studies, and other data that can stand up to scrutiny. Always have two people to compare in any hiring decision, and remember: Don't buy the hype that you're "leaving money on the table" by not buying into the latest thing. In the end, all of these things are fads. Even the Internet. A couple of hundred years from now, if the Internet as we know it still exists, we'll have failed as a species.

+ The easiest way to spot the frauds is to look at how they react when you challenge them. If they call you a dinosaur? They're a fraud. People who are confident in what they know will sit down and have a conversation with you that doesn't involve outrageous superlatives like "engage or die." They also won't be afraid to be wrong. So, let me take a moment to say this now: I don't know everything. This is what I've found from my own experience and research. I could be wrong.

+ None of these platforms are great for business. Twitter has some usefulness for connecting with strangers, and if you live in a place like New York where it's impossible to break out and get attention through the press, it doesn't hurt to be using it—there's a critical mass of users in the area. But that doesn't apply to the places most of us live. We live in places where radio and print remain the most effective form of advertisement, which is why the Cyber Hipsters and marketers (many based out of large cities) hate radio and print. For them, it doesn't work. They live in specific settings, but write as if what's true in those settings is true for the rest of us.

Next time you pick up a business or marketing book (or even something about the Internet) look carefully at where that author is from. In my case, I live in upstate New York, which is a close reflection of pretty much everywhere in America that's not NY, LA, and SF.

- You don't need to use *any* of these platforms. It all comes down to what you're looking to do and who your audience is. Telling people that they're losing money by not using "social media" is a lie made up by marketers of all stripes to sell you bullshit that's going to benefit them. The only thing you need is a Web site. One that's clean, simple, easy to navigate, fast to load, and fun. That sounds like a tall order, but it's not. And a Web site won't cost you a fortune, either, aside potentially from the domain name (which you should keep short and register for as many years as you can afford. The minimum is two.). You should also consider having a self-hosted Wordpress blog. It's something that *you* control. You're not at the mercy of another company that can delete you or go down at any moment. Hosts like ZippyKid.com, which I use, are cheap, reliable, and they'll set you up with a self-hosted Wordpress blog. That's where you should start, and that's where you should focus your efforts. Any and all traffic you get should go to your Web site. You own it, and long after Facebook bites the dust, it'll still be there.

- Everything that happens on the Web is driven by the media. The idea that there are limitless choices and millions of alternatives online is bullshit. We spend most, if not all of, our time with corporate owned Web sites, and although there are millions of blogs and "social media" users out there, all of the information they get is coming from a consolidated group of places that are almost exclusively under corporate ownership. So if something happens on television, it's big on Twitter. *Not the other way around.* This also means that if you want to succeed in whatever it is that you do, you need the media, not "the people formerly known as the audience" or "influencers."

- "Social media" is bullshit. Search engine optimization is not. But, SEO isn't going to solve all your problems, either. That industry is filled with just as many assholes as the "social media" industry, and most of what they're selling you can figure out on your own: Build in-bound links to your Web site that use key words associated with whatever you're doing (Google loves links from the media) and post frequently. The more content (posts, pictures, and video), appropriately tagged, the better.

- Did you ever notice that the people who want to sell you on the idea of "influencers" portray themselves as influencers themselves? That's not a coincidence. Although there are people out there who have the power to make or break you, and this is true on community news Web sites like Reddit, targeting those people and figuring out who actually has that power is a fool's errand. You'll also find that the alleged influence of the influencers is negligible. For example, you may see a nice short-term spike in traffic if a big Web site links to you, but if that traffic goes away and nobody sticks around, it's not exactly doing you any favors. If you get the media behind you, the people with real power will see what you're doing and, like everyone else, pass on what you're doing, without your involvement. Remember: Your presence on these different platforms, with an extreme exception here or there, *is redundant.* If people like what you do, they'll do the work of sharing it for you, as long as you've made it easy for them to do so.

+ Analysts like to repackage what they've read elsewhere and then sell it to corporations at outrageously marked-up prices. If the analysts are saying it, you're too late to be "ahead of the curve." So essentially they have a scam going where they're taking advantage of people, both the companies and the rest of us by selling "insight" into things that are already past their expiration date. Unfortunately, there are not many "good" sources of information that you can go to in order to bypass the analysts when it comes to tech news. They're not perfect, but I recommend you go to Techmeme.com, which aggregates all the big tech stories in one place and (usually) filters out the bad stuff. Just look out for Cyber Hipsters, their bullshit often clogs up Techmeme.com and keeps it from being a must-visit destination.

+ Everyone wants to be accepted. That's why sales tactics for "social media" that involve making people feel left out if they don't adopt the latest platform are so effective. That's why so much credence is given to the Cyber Hipsters I've described. Even if what they say is patently false, there are a lot of people out there who don't have answers about the Web, who see Cyber Hipsters talking their bullshit, and so they just follow the leader. *Don't follow the leader.* The Cyber Hipsters don't know what they're talking about, either. The only answers you're ever going to need are the ones your audience tells you and the ones your choose for yourself. Most of this stuff that you see packaged and sold as expertise is guesswork. For more on that, you should read David Freeman's *Wrong: Why Experts Keep Failing Us and How to Know When Not to Trust Them.*

+ The 1 Percent Rule: The parties I've mentioned in this book all talk about "everybody," "the people formerly known as the audience," "the community," stuff like that. This is bullshit. The Web and the other Internet-based platforms are *niche mediums*, meaning the people *you* interact with will not represent *everybody*. In some cases, again based on your needs and desires as well as what you're selling, that might be fine. But. Since 1997, it's been well documented that a small minority of users do the majority of the talking on the Web while the rest of us just listen. It is incredibly dangerous, and foolish, to believe that this 1 percent is reflective of entire societies and cultures. Remember: It was the rich—the one in eight Egyptians—who were responsible for organizing the Facebook protest, but it was only because the poor were involved, *the seven in eight without Internet access*, that those early protests were successful. Ok. That . . . and the Egyptian military let the protests happen. That was the key component in Egypt, not the Internet. If the military had gotten involved, Egypt would have wound up like Syria or Libya. In Libya's case, it took out help to overthrow Gaddafi. So, don't lose any sleep over bad comments made about you on the Internet, and don't buy the hype about the Internet, either. "The people," as they've so often been described, don't exist.

And that, my friends, brings us to failure, and the final chapter of this book.

## CHAPTER NINETEEN

# THE ANTI-SOCIAL MEDIA MANIFESTO

---

**IN OUR DARKER MOMENTS** we have our best epiphanies. The good news is that those moments are few and far between. The bad news is that, because they happen so infrequently, the moments of clarity that come with them are also uncommon. In our usual, hazier state, it can be relatively easy for bullshit to take root.

It's not just you, don't worry. It happens to everyone, myself included. And it's not until something happens, usually something challenging, that we come to our senses. That's what happened to me. I was a hardcore believer in "social media." I wrote articles about it, I praised all the people I told you about in this book, and I did everything they said to do. None of it worked, but I still wanted to believe it did.

## ROSWELL THAT ENDS WELL

In January of 2009, against all common sense, reason, and sage advice from everyone involved, my wife and I embarked on a cross-country tour to raise money for a small not-for-profit I was working for. I was tasked with coming up with a way to get college-aged students to check themselves more frequently to help catch and treat cancer early. The slogan I took with me to college campuses across America? "Check early and check often." My mission? Raise five million dollars for the small not-for-profit. But by the time my wife and I arrived in Roswell, New Mexico, on what had become an Odyssey-like adventure that even Homer wouldn't believe, we were in bad shape. Our car was dying, and our tour was a failure.

Our plan to raise the five million dollars was to ask my growing number of Twitter followers to donate five dollars to the small not-for-profit. In the run-up to the tour I had created a Twitter account, @BJMendelson, and grew the number of followers I had to three thousand in less than three months. As word got around about the tour, the number of followers we had started to grow, and I was confident that they were going to work with me in making this tour a successful one. Before leaving for the tour, I had made a pitch to Twitter about using their platform as a vehicle for getting the word out. In late 2007 and early 2008 I had made heavy use of the service for a proposed project with MTV, Facebook, YouTube, and others that ultimately fell through, and Twitter was kind enough to promote my account on their old public timeline. I figured they'd be willing to do it again for a good cause. What I didn't know was *how* Twitter was going to promote the @BJMendelson account. They never replied to my e-mail. Instead, as had quickly become par for the course with the tour, something amazing (on a superficial level) had happened: During our tour stop at Raleigh, North Carolina, Twitter debuted their now-defunct "Suggested User List." I was the only non-brand, non-celebrity, non-media outlet on the list, which immediately made me a public enemy to the Cyber Hipsters. But while I brushed off the slings and arrows from guys like Loic Lemeceur, Robert Scoble, and Leo Laparte like a *Biggest Loser* contestant when they have to stand around on that scale with their shirt off, thanks to the list I went from a few thousand followers to fifty thousand, and climbing, almost overnight. Emboldened by all my new followers, and the idea that it'd be way easier now to get them to participate in the tour, my wife and I pressed on instead of going home.

But not a single one of those new followers donated to the not-for-profit. In fact, the grand total of donations Amanda and I had after we were placed on the Suggested User List was a dollar. Not only didn't these "followers" not donate, but when I invited them to come out and meet with me on our tour, only three took me up on it. I know my beard sometimes gives off a creepy vibe, like that of a pedophile in the midst of an evening stroll, but something tells me a pedophile probably could have drawn more attention than we did . . . at least from law-enforcement officials. And this was even *after* the official Dunkin' Donuts Twitter feed promoted several of our tour meet-ups in places like Washington, D.C.

When I talked to my friends in the "social media" field about this, they all said the same thing: "That's not how 'social media' works." "You can't expect your followers to do stuff like that."

Well, isn't that how it's supposed to work? What's the point of having a million followers when none of them are clicking on your links (they weren't), following your calls to actions (they also weren't), and not coming out to meet you (ditto)? Isn't that *exactly* the effect your "social media" efforts are *supposed* to have? Even if you assume 99.9 percent of the one million followers that I had at one point (the account, like others on the Suggested User List, has since declined and continues to do so) were spam, that's still one thousand people who weren't, and that would be in addition to the three thousand or so followers that I spent hours networking with, retweeting, @replying, and otherwise stalking prior to the debut of the Suggested User List. You'd think we would have seen way more activity, but we didn't. We saw almost nothing. And it wasn't just Twitter that wasn't delivering the goods. We were everywhere on every service doing everything you've ever been told to do by the "social media" marketers, and nothing was happening.

I couldn't have known how some of these ideas were going to play out when I was in Roswell though. I didn't have the luxury of hindsight. But these thoughts started creeping into the back of my mind while we were there. When the guy at the Jiffy Lube popped open the hood, took a look at our transmission, and revealed a dipstick coated in a curious jet-black substance, I couldn't help but wonder, "Why aren't all these followers participating in the crowd-funding efforts for this tour?" When we went to the Chevy dealership to see what was wrong with the car and they told us it was a risk to continue driving it, I couldn't help but think, "My Twitter account was shown in a segment on the *ABC Evening News*. What's the deal?" And when my wife, Amanda, and I went to a shady junkyard looking for a cheap used car that we could trade our dying Impala for (and after wasting hours there until the owner called and said he didn't want it), I thought, *They don't click on anything, either.*

I managed to suppress these thoughts until we found ourselves back in the dying car, driving in darkness between Roswell and Albuquerque. Common sense and reason hadn't kicked in yet. Amanda and I did the drive in complete silence. In between thoughts of "We're going to die" and "Social Media is bullshit," everything that I had been suppressing as doubts about "social media" since 2007 boiled to the surface.

"If the 1 Percent Rule is true, who are those people, and are they worth the time, money, and energy to pursue?"

"Why do the other 99 percent do nothing? Aren't they supposed to be active sharers and publishers who are changing everything?"

"The Internet is pretty liberal. The people who do the bulk of the publishing we consume are well educated, white, and a lot of them went to fancy private colleges. That doesn't describe 'everyone' at all."

"The only people who seem fascinated by the number of followers, fans, likes, views, and the number of times something has been downloaded are the media."

"Come to think of it, there are an awful lot of people getting rich by selling advice on how to get more of those, but I just don't see anyone actually getting rich beyond them."

Then I started to think about the International UFO Museum and Research Center. When Amanda and I weren't on college campuses trying to tell college students to "check early and check often," we were filming these small "microupdates," sponsored by Sprint, where we would do fun things around the places we visited. In Roswell, the museum was our destination.

I had built up the museum in my mind. I thought it would be this huge place like the New York State museum in Albany and have all sorts of cool stuff about aliens, but . . . well, let's just say that, like the promise of "social media," it didn't live up to my expectations. We tend to make places we've never been and people we'll never meet bigger and better in our minds than they actually are. I had never been to Roswell, New Mexico, so I had no frame of reference beyond a show that aired on UPN after *Buffy* that only got better after Commander William Riker started directing it. So in the absence of something concrete, I started to draw my own conclusions as to what the place would be like.

In the absence of the truth, we do the same with things like "social media." We don't know what it actually is—as it turns out, it isn't anything, just a buzzword, a buzzword made up by marketers and their friends. But we don't *know* that because we have no frame of reference other than what is being told to us by these individuals and the media. And since the media is more concerned with hype than facts, we get excited about the things they hype (that same vicious cycle Gawker's Hamilton Nolan talked about earlier).

What's missing from this equation, and it has been missing since the Web took off as a potential medium for people to "make their dreams come true" on, is something to ground these thoughts and ideas in reality. There are not many people who have stepped forward to say that "social media is bullshit." It's not a narrative currently accepted by the media. So out of those thoughts, in one of my darker moments when we were roaming the vast emptiness of New Mexico in a car that could have died at any moment, leaving us stranded and with no cell service, the idea for this book developed. It was originally going to be called *Soap Box Included*, and I was going to talk about something I called "social publishing." But even as I started to develop the idea, I still clung on to the remnants of these myths. I wanted to believe that they were true— that the myth of "social media" could deliver on its promise despite a growing body of evidence to suggest that simply wasn't the case and never was.

It's hard to let go of an idea, especially when everyone else believes it. Just like with "Nickelback Syndrome." Nickelback Syndrome is one of the best reasons the myth of "social media" has been successful in spreading.

## SAYING "FAIL" IS A FAIL. STOP SAYING IT.

The breast cancer tour was the seventh failed project of mine in as many years. Each time I'd take what I learned from all of these marketing books and these other sources, and each time I would be disappointed. I never let those failures get to me. The only time that happened was that moment between Roswell and Albuquerque. And in that moment, I looked back at all the failures I had using this stuff. This didn't mean that the platforms were bad or that I was doing it wrong. It was the *advice I was given that was wrong*. And with the way the economy is, and has been for much of the last ten years, we just can't afford to keep getting and repeating that bad advice. The era of bad advice about how to "make it" on the Web must come to an end. And that starts not just by calling out the "social media" experts, but by calling out the term itself.

As I've laid out for you throughout this book, "the game" you keep hearing about is rigged. Nothing has changed. An exciting new medium came along, and as it happened with the telephone, radio, television, and cable, it quickly became dominated by some of the most powerful corporations in the world. The promise that was implied by these mediums created a dilemma, the likes of which hasn't been seen since "Sophie's Choice." On the one hand, there was an opportunity that looked great on paper, that you could use any of these platforms to make your dreams come true. But, the actual odds of doing so got worse as time went on, and as more of the big corporations began to dominate the different avenues the Internet and Web have to offer. They squeezed out the smaller players. The Internet and Web, as it was commonly portrayed, was different from the way it was in reality. Although it's a noble concept to suggest the audience is now the producer, that's only true for a small class of people; the rest of us are still an audience, and one that's using the Web to respond to what we experience *offline*. It's things like the media that are driving what's happening online, not the other way around. You know, the one before they all decided not to shower. The media driving the conversation won't change because the Web is a platform for niche audiences, and not the masses, and business models depending on niche audiences can only work if that niche is large enough to sustain them. In most cases? It's not. So instead, you get more of the same that you could find on other mediums because only the well-funded and corporate can survive.

And so, because we're responding online to what we see offline, and because the corporations control the platforms and reap the benefit from your work, we find ourselves back in the same position we were before the Web got here: nowhere, except now those companies are making money by slapping ads next to your stuff and getting all the traffic and attention that should be going to your Web site.

So what do you do? Especially in the incredibly likely event that you're going to fail? Get-rich-quick schemes like "social media" come and go.

I have a plan: or at least, a suggestion. Come up with an idea; it doesn't even have to be a good one. You then go and see how people respond to that idea. If they love it or hate it? You've got a winner. If they're indifferent? Then you need to come up with something else. The important thing is that they have an opinion on it. You take that idea and research it. Who else is doing what you're doing? Can you do it better? If no one else is doing it, find out why? Do they know something you don't? Then you go and talk to the people at the Small Business Administration and SCORE and do more research. I can't stress this enough to you: DO THE RESEARCH. Know your potential audience. Know your area. Your circumstances. Your limitations. "Social Media" was a success as a get-rich-quick scheme because of all the things we DON'T know. The more you know, the more you can get done, and done right, without falling prey to bullshit. What you'll find in doing your research, and never stopping, is that you'll have a clearer picture of what you need and room to try different things. Is Twitter right for you? I don't know. You figure it out. Remember? And if you do your research, you'll know the answer to that and all the other questions the marketers and their friends want you to pay them to answer.

Failure can be crippling. Failure keeps us from doing the work and trying new things. It makes us prone to believing that if the "experts" and everyone else is saying something, they must be right. They're not. The experts are almost always wrong. That's why I'm glad I'm not one. I'm just a guy who wasted years of his life and untold thousands on bad ideas, bad strategies, and bad advice because I wanted to make my dreams come true using the Internet.

Given the choice between giving up and driving into the unknown, Amanda and I drove into the unknown, knowing full well that we were in a strange place with no cell reception and a dying car. Should you do that exact same thing? No! But you should take the motivation behind that and apply it. You're driving into the unknown. No one knows how it's going to turn out. Not me. Not Seth Godin. Not Clay Shirky. Not Mene Gene Oaklerland and his infamous 1-900 number. No one. But if you do your research and ask questions, you'll be prepared for when you fail. And that's a totally acceptable thing. Failure isn't good. You shouldn't "embrace failure." But it's also not something to fear. Failure is just something that happens. How prepared you are will determine its impact on you. If you're prepared for failure, you're going to be fine. So don't let it cripple you.

When I say "make it" and "break out" in this book, I'm referring very simply to the idea that you've achieved whatever your goals are. To me, "make it" means you're able to pay your bills and put some of what you make into savings. That, to me, is success, and that's the kind of thing we should all be striving for. But you're not going to make that happen by wasting money. Advertising is *not* a waste of money. It's easy to measure and utilizes a metric anyone can understand—Did you make money or lose it? "Social media" is a waste of money. So are most marketing efforts. "Social media" doesn't work, and beyond that, it doesn't in any real sense even exist. The same can be said about marketing. Marketing is a fiction created by salesmen to get companies to buy ideas they don't need, to sell customers what they don't want, to an end that only benefits their own.

What it all comes down to is your ideas, your research, your audience, and your specific set of circumstances. Maybe "social media" works if you have limitless resources. But what does that mean for the rest of us? We should save our money, ignore the "experts," and stick to what works—the traditional stuff I told you about in Chapter 17. Maybe in the next book we can figure it out together.

## THE END

There's one last thing I want to leave you with before you put this book down. I'm *not* saying that you *can't* use something like Twitter and become rich and famous. Although there were a lot of external factors involved, Shit My Dad Says did come from a Twitter account. Ditto for Justin Bieber. Although there were a lot of external factors involved, he did ultimately break out due to a video he placed *on* YouTube. I can't dispute that. But those external factors are often ignored in all of these "social media success stories," and in the end, those external factors are the things that matter most. Without them, we wouldn't be talking about Justin in the first place.

Even if you disagree with pretty much everything I've said so far, I challenge you to look closely at any Internet or "social media success stories" and to question them. There *are* legitimate stories of success out there. Maddox, of The Best Page in The Universe, is a great example of this. He had a really funny Web site, people wanted to pass on his articles to their friends, and the thing took off from there, eventually landing Maddox on *The New York Times* bestseller list. Those things can happen, but they're incredibly rare. Instead what we find in almost all of the cases of "social media success stories," the people are rich or well connected (or both), often white, and come from highly wired areas such as San Francisco, Palo Alto, or New York City. And as the Web has gone corporate, organic success stories like Maddox's are rare, if not extinct. Instead, people will become successful based on who they know and the business interests of these companies. Just like any other medium.

You might be thinking, Who cares *how* they got famous, they're still "social media success stories." Well, you should care. Because the organic things that break out on the Web are few and far between. Instead, we're seeing a small elite rewarded while the rest of us are putting our money toward implementing advice that isn't geared toward us in the first place

The experts say that "social media" is putting power into the hands of the people. That "monologue is giving way to dialogue." And that these newly empowered people are going to change everything. None of this is true. We have less power, not more, and nobody is listening to what we have to say unless companies, the media, or someone famous gets involved. Wall Street does this all the time when they want to avoid regulation, as do the big tech companies like Google and Facebook. (As you saw with the SOPA protests). If we're going to succeed, not just in whatever our business and marketing goals are, but in life, then we need to clean this mess up and get the truth out. And the truth is this: The Web and these platforms don't work as advertised; it has been corrupted by the same groups that have corrupted the other media. We live in a world where you can make far more money telling people about how to get rich on the Internet than you can by actually trying to get rich. That needs to change.

We can't clean up this mess until we stand up to the "experts"—the marketers who act no different than those football players back when I was in high school. They're bullies. And they're bullies enriching themselves off of fear and misinformation. As long as we turn a blind eye to that—as long as we suppress those thoughts that tell us the emperor is wearing no clothes, like I did—we will continue to find ourselves frustrated that we're not reaching our goals. As long as we accept the myth, the truth remains buried, and none of us are going to succeed.

I'm not a marketer. The height of my ambition is telling jokes in front of a brick wall at a dive bar in a place like Spread Eagle, Wisconsin. I don't profess to know everything, but as a wannabe comedian, I've learned that the best jokes (and the best writing) comes from saying what everyone else is thinking. I've done that here. I've told you the truth many of your colleagues and friends already know. Unfortunately, there are many, many more out there who don't know the truth and it's our responsibility. We're all going to drive into the unknown someday, and if we can make that ride for our friends and neighbors a smooth one, I believe we have the obligation to do so. So, spread the word. Don't assume someone else is going to do it for you:

Social media is bullshit. Q.E.D.

# ACKNOWLEDGMENTS

At the top of the list of people I want to thank? Joan Rivers. If it wasn't for an amorous, alcohol-fueled encounter between my mother and father after a Joan Rivers performance, I wouldn't be here, and you wouldn't be reading this.

I'd also like to thank my mom and dad. As you'll learn more about me (thanks to a Wikipedia page I better get), you'll know my family history is a little dark. Just like that Wonder Woman joke. Things are much, much better now, and I think that's a testament to my parents and humanity in general. Things suck, you deal with it, and then you adapt and grow from there. That's what they and I did, and we're all better people for it. I love my parents, and I'm happy they and the rest of the family are part of my life.

There are a lot of teachers I'd like to thank, starting with Mrs. Carmen in the Monroe-Woodbury Middle School to Mr. Romeo, Loalbo, and McTammeny at the high school, to Dr. Constantine, Barwick, and Laubert at Alfred State, and finally to Dr. Neisser, Dr. Massaro, and Dr. Del Guidice at SUNY Potsdam. Although in Dr. Del

Guidice's case, I'm convinced I drove him into an early retirement. One other teacher I want to single out is Mr. Dames from Monroe-Woodbury Senior High School. I took an AP European History course my senior year for all the wrong reasons and then got stuck in it, so I just phoned it in despite the fact that I actually enjoy history. At the end of the year Mr. Dames said to me, "Mr. Mendelson, if you do work in life like you did in this class, you're going to spend the rest of your life bagging groceries." It took a few years for that to sink in, but when it did, it changed my work ethic completely. Consequently, I have Mr. Dames to blame for my workaholism.

(Oh, and if not for Mr. Dames, I would have potentially been murdered by angry football players upon their discovery of The Island.)

I'm probably forgetting some very important people, but many teachers contributed to helping me be a better writer than I started out as. Seriously. You should visit the Way Back Machine at Archive.org and search for thebrandonshow.com. Some of my old stuff is on there, and it's horrible. Let's just say I was really into *Fight Club* and *The Matrix* at that time.

I'd also like to thank Amanda Morin and her family. They must have thought I was crazy when I told them about the breast cancer tour and some of the other things I've tried to pull off since she and I have been together. It'll be seven years by the time you're reading this. I'm glad this book came out almost exclusively because it'll be the first time I said I was going to do something big, and then it happened. So whether or not this thing sells, I've already won. Now when Amanda says something like, "You always say you're going to do something and then never do it," I can say, "Hey, remember that time I said I was going to write a book?"

Amanda, her brother Kyle, Amanda's sister-in-law Cindy, and her parents, Mark and Wendy Morin, are awesome, and since Day 2 (Day 1 was blown when I couldn't figure out how to open a TV tray and

Amanda's Dad yelled at me), they've treated me like family. I've always appreciated that, especially given my family situation being the way it was. (I also want to thank Amanda's Mom, Wendy, for being the first person to read *Social Media Is Bullshit*, giving me honest feedback, and even suggestions on how to make it better. She's very busy, and for her to give up her free time when coming home from work to look at this meant a lot to me.)

As far as this book goes, as you might have guessed, it was insanely difficult to get people to talk to me. They either thought it was a straight-up humor book, or that I was just being an asshole. Both are fair points. There were some folks like Matthew Inman from The Oatmeal and NPR's Andy Carvin, both of whom said they would do an interview, and then when I sent them the questions, I never heard from them again. That was actually the case with a lot of "Web celebrities." I found the reason they became popular, and when I went to ask them about it, I got stonewalled. I was most disappointed with Carvin, though. He DM'ed me on Twitter saying he liked the title and thought "social media" was bullshit, but then he got a book deal about tweeting and the Arab Spring, and then like that, I never heard from him again.

But where they stepped down, others like Ryan Holiday and Felicia Williams stepped up, and for that, I'm thankful.

Aside from a lot of "Web celebrities," many people were really generous with their time. Guys I thought wouldn't be because I took issue with some of the stuff they've said. Jeff Jarvis spent almost two hours on the phone with me, as did Gary Vaynerchuk. That's the kind of thing I like. I don't hate these guys, I just disagree with some of the things that they've said, so being able to actually talk to them humanized them in a way that otherwise would be impossible if I had just read their work on the Web. It's really easy to hate Jeff Jarvis if you just read his writing. I'm the same way. I sound like a dick. But then you actually talk to the guy and you go, "Oh, you're a person like me and you're kind of cool" and everything changes. I still have issues with some of what these guys say, but I like being able to disagree in a way that's entertaining (for you) but also intellectually interesting (for me). That kind of thing is nice, especially because we're all an Xbox Live game away from an overprivileged thirteen-year-old calling you a name I can't print.

I'd like to thank my anonymous sources. Also Mark Hopkins, Jimmy Wales, James Erwin, Eric Becker, Sir Tim Berners-Lee, Professor William Laubert, Professor John Massaro, Brooklyn Borough President Marty Markowitz, Chase Norlin, Andrew Keen, Jonathon Green, Tucker Max, Drew Curtis, Maddox, Tim Ferriss, Vince Mancini, Paul from TheHighDefinite.com, Nick Carr, Loren Feldman, Hamilton Nolan, Steve Hicks, Marc Maron, Dr. Robert Thompson, Dr. Judith Klienfeld, Dr. Duncan Watts, Dr. Harry Frankfurt, Dr. Simon J. Bronner, Dr. David Armitage, Dr. Jakob Nielsen, Dean McBeth, Tony Shieh, Rebbecca Blood, Evan Williams, Dan Lyons, Scott E. Fahlman, Jacquie Jordan, Evan White, Calvin Martin, Nathan Hirst, Adam Carolla, Rob Corddry, Liz Shannon Miller, Felicia Williams, Richard Cleland, Lizz Winstead, Justin Halpern, Jon Weissman, Danny Sullivan, Michael Eliran, Andrew Sorcini, Roberta Rosenberg, Nick Douglas, Jake Sasseville, Michael D'Antonio, Susan Giese, Fred Wilson, David Bohnett, Brad from the band Dispatch, Gabriel Weinberg, Kalle Lasn, Jeff Bercovici, Tim Bray, Jeffrey Harmon, and Tron Guy. Not everyone's insights made it into the final manuscript, but all of them helped to shape the overall tone, message, and points I made.

(Other points that were shared with me, like from "Rome Sweet Rome" creator James Erwin, Maddox, and Tim Ferriss were too awesome to be contained in just this one book. You should visit BJMendelson.com to see the full interviews I did with them.)

I'd also like to thank Andrew Meader at Applause Factory, Amanda Magee at Trampoline Design, Stephen at GorillaMask, Josh Karp at

The Printed Block, Steve Huff, Jared Brickman (a fellow SUNY Potsdam alum), Jason Sanders, Chris at DogAndPonyShow.com, Scott Kramer (former New Media Director for Lopez Tonight), and Joseph Cannizzaro for reading through the book in different stages and giving me feedback.

I'd also like to thank good friends and some good people including Ed Thomas, Mike Thompson, Tara Dublin, Robert Taylor, Colonel John Folsom, Vince from Film Drunk, Chris Menning, Mike Huber, Scott Kostloni, Derek Meister, and Leon Henderson.

Also: Comic artist Rusty Shackles (aka Jay King) did an awesome cover for this book that you'll never get to see, but don't worry, we're going to be doing other stuff together for you to enjoy in the not too distant future. If all goes according to plan, you might have already saw some of it by now . . .

And how can I not mention Greg R. Goldstein and his invaluable assistance, time, and patience throughout the years? Aside from my family, Greg has known me the longest and has worked with me on pretty much every insane idea I've had. When I wanted to buy the old Clarkson University campus in downtown Potsdam, Greg was there. When I decided to travel across America with no budget in an attempt to raise five million dollars for a breast cancer charity using "social media," Greg was there, and even today when I'm talking to him about buying a radio station and turning it into a "Radio Comedy Central," Greg has been there.

Oh, and then there was the time I was being trolled hard on the Internet by an eighty-seven-year-old woman dying of cancer. Greg was there for that one, too.

I haven't known Dan Mandel, my agent at Sanford J. Greenburger, as long as Greg, but Dan is a welcome addition to the family, and I couldn't be happier to be working with him. I like that Dan is patient with me, especially because during this whole process from writing a book proposal through writing the book, to even now through the production process, I've been a total basket case. Not because I'm hung up on how the book will do, but because I've never done anything like this, and as romanticized as writers envision the book writing process to be, we are so totally unprepared for what the process is actually like, that it's ridiculous. It's like putting your dog in front of a typewriter and saying to it, "you figure it out." And all those books you read about how to write a book? They're bullshit, too. What every writer needs isn't a book like that, they need a Dan Mandel to steer them in the right direction. I also think Greg is thankful for Dan being around because it's taken the crazy-shit burden off of him for a while.

And finally, I'd like to thank the team at St. Martin's Press, starting with Yaniv Soha, who was great to work with. I probably drove the team there crazy making requests like, "Let's put the e-book on sale for $1," but this book wouldn't be in the shape that it's in if not for Yaniv working with me and patiently dealing with the occasional OCD-inspired editorial madness I suffer from. I tend to stick to working with people I like, so I hope to work with Yaniv and St. Martin's again in the future.

Until such a time that you require a book that makes you think while you're going to the bathroom, I'll smell you, and whatever it is you're doing in there, later.

# ENDNOTES

## Chapter 1

1. GeoCities was one of the Web's most popular Web sites throughout the 1990s. It felt like everyone had a page on there, and a lot of that had to do with how easy it was to set up a Web site. According to what the site's founder, David Bohnett, told me, for the early part of its existence GeoCities had premade templates people could use for their Web sites, and then in 1996 (or 1997, he wasn't sure) they rolled out a What You See Is What You Get editor (WYSIWYG) to make putting up a Web site as simple as editing a text document in Word. If I had known about GeoCities, I would have used it instead of using the iMac and Microsoft Word.

2. Any "dialogue" from Whitey is as best as I can remember. I spoke to him briefly about this section of the book, but for professional reasons, he didn't want to comment about "The Island." As you might have guessed, "Whitey" isn't his real name, either. I also spoke to former classmates

Brian Egan, Don Bayne, Jim O'Shea, Rita Hosdaghian, Miguel Garcia, and Heather Clayton to vouch for the accurateness of this chapter.

3. Although I'm not a fan of most buzzwords and marketing phrases, I don't mind "going viral" because, at its core, it's a phrase that reflects a desire for something to spread online, organically, and as a culture, we all seem to have accepted that definition. Although it's exceedingly rare for something to "go viral" in an organic or legitimate sense, it *can* happen. Unfortunately, this phrase has also been co-opted and drained of all meaning by the marketers and their friends to refer to things that spread for less legit reasons. So when I say "go viral" in this book, I'm referring purely to the *organic* and legitimate sense of something spreading online, without the involvement of a celebrity, media, or anything of that nature. Metallica's growth, as a result of fans trading tapes in the '80s, is a great example of viral growth in an organic and legitimate sense.

## Chapter 2

1. As far as I know, I am still banned from WETD at Alfred State College. I left so much of an impression on them that I've been told the station advisors still talk trash about me. So, let me take a moment to apologize to Mark Amman and Rick Herritt, the adult supervision at the station: I was an asshole. I apologize.

2. Edward L. Bernays, widely considered to be the father of public relations, said "It's easier to gain acceptance for your viewpoint by quoting respected authorities, outlining the reasons for your outlook, and referring to tradition than by telling someone he's wrong." I recommend reading *The Father of Spin: Edward L. Bernays and the Birth of PR* for more about him. Like Dale Carnegie, you're going to find a lot of stuff from Bernays that has been repackaged and sold today, using new buzzwords. In fact,

I'll go as far as telling you that the only books about PR that you should read are *Crystallizing Public Opinion* and *Propaganda,* both by Bernays. (And for the record? *Crystallizing* came out in 1923; *Propaganda* in 1928.)

3. William Laubert, associate professor of speech communication, Alfred State College, in discussion with the author, August 2011.

## Chapter 3

1. That social media books are padded with filler is the chief complaint if you look at the reviews on Amazon. Of course . . . if you were to look at the reviews on Amazon you'll also find a ton loaded with five star ratings, suspiciously by people with a newly registered Amazon account, with nothing but glowing things to say about the author, something we addressed later in this book.

2. Marketing is not advertising. So while all marketing is bullshit beyond the four items I mention, advertising is an important, and critical, part of anyone's success. As Jeffrey Harmon, the CMO at Orabrush told me about what made the Orabrush videos successfully spread on YouTube, "Everyone is so enamored with the buzzword 'viral' that they are blinded to the fact that we spend money on ads to push the ad." Advertising isn't a cure-all, either, but you can measure the results of an ad campaign better than you can with marketing, and when you're working with no budget, that makes all the difference.

3. The following is often attributed to Albert Einstein: "You do not really understand something unless you can explain it to your grandmother." It's not clear if he actually said it—you can see Wikiquote's attempt to track down the original quotation and its source here: http://en.wikiquote.org/wiki/Albert_Einstein.

4. Shannon Geise at the Altimeter Group explained their definition of an enterprise class corporation to me: "We're using a standard definition of an Enterprise Class as a company with over 1,000 employees. This same standard is applied at other research firms, including how we used this at Forrester Research. Why employee size? Revenue isn't always available, nor a reflection of maturity of early and growing companies."

5. These numbers come from Facebook by way of AllFacebook.com's Facebook Pages Leaderboard: http://statistics.allfacebook.com/pages /leaderboard/-/-/-/f/DESC//-

6. You can find a frequently updated list of the most popular Twitter users, by followers, at http://twitaholic.com/

7. Amir Efrati, "Top 50 Youtube Channels Revealed," *The Wall Street Journal*. September 22, 2011. http://blogs.wsj.com/digits/2011/09/22/ top-50-youtube-channels-revealed/

8. The Top 10 Web Brands, according to Nielsen, as of August 2011 were: (1) Google (2) Facebook (3) Yahoo! (4) MSN / Windows Live / Bing (5) YouTube (Google) (6) Microsoft (7) AOL's network of Web sites (8) Wikipedia (9) Amazon (10) Apple. You can find the list, as well as a breakdown of how Americans were using the Internet in August 2011 here: http://blog.nielsen.com/nielsenwire/online_mobile/august -2011-top-us-web-brands/

9. Wesley W. Neff, the president of the Leigh Bureau, who handles Malcolm Gladwell's speaking dates, declined to reveal to me what the actual numbers are. The book, *Confessions of a Public Speaker*, which I highly recommend, places the amount Gladwell charges corporations at $80,000, but reports on the Web often cite it as being closer to $90,000.

10. I don't like the term "Cyber-utopians" because it's a very narrow classification and assumes that they're all simple-minded in how they perceive the world and want it to be. I'm guilty of doing some similar reduction, so let me issue an all-purpose caveat here: Not all marketers are bad. Ditto with Cyber Hipsters, Cyber-utopians, analysts, politicians, and any other party I might have mocked over the course of this book.

11. Harry G. Frankfurt, *On Bullshit*. (Princeton University Press, 2005).

12. Ibid, 56.

## Chapter 4

1. This e-mail is a composite of messages I received in response to Gary Vaynerchuk's second book. The quote from Gary's book is real. You can find it in Chapter 1 under "Engagement Is Not a Four-Letter Word."

2. I talked with Gary for about two hours for this book. I've been a fan of his since 2008, and I want to be clear that I'm not taking shots at him. I think if people need a little extra motivation, there's nothing wrong with offering it. I also don't think Gary is a bad marketer; he's actually one of the good ones. You know why? Because he has a track record of proven *financial* success with his projects. That said, I want to share with you an exchange I had with Gary about the use of the term "social media" in that passage I showed you in this chapter. When I asked Gary what his definition of "social media" was, he told me, "It's the Internet." He added, "It's the modern word for it. It's the new word. You know the word that got me into this world was Web 2.0. Remember? You know what social media is? It's Web 2.0. You know what Web 2.0 was? It was the Internet. It is the maturity of the Internet itself. I don't give a rat's ass about Facebook, or Twitter or Tumblr or Ustream or Klout or Foursquare. This is the

greatest platform in human history and people are building smarter things on top of it that are connecting us and thus they had to create a word for it. The reason everyone sucks at it is because of the word "media." The second they hear media they think content and push. What connecting people is, is about listening and engaging." I agree with Gary on this part, and he reminded me of something Jeff Jarvis, professor at the CUNY Graduate School of Journalism and cocreator of *Entertainment Weekly*, told me that summed things up the best, "It's not about social media, it's about people." Jarvis added, "The simple message here is that you have new ways to listen to your public, your customers, your constituents, whoever. And if you don't listen to them, interact with them, collaborate with them, you're a damn fool. That to me is the essence of what 'social media' gets to." If Gary had said, "The Internet" instead of "social media" in his statement from *The Thank You Economy*, it would be absolutely right. It's narrowing the field to "social media" that keeps that statement from being true, for reasons I outline in this book.

3. Joseph Jaffe, in conversation with the author, October 2011.


## Chapter 5

1. Julia, Angwin, *Stealing MySpace: The Battle to Control the Most Popular Website in America* (New York: Random House, 2009).

2. Daniel Roth, "Time Your Attack: Oracle's Lost Revolution," *Wired*. December 21, 2009. http://www.wired.com/magazine/2009/12/fail_oracle/all/1

3. Nicholas Carr, "Cloud Computing, circa 1965," *Rough Type*. November 28, 2009. http://www.roughtype.com/archives/2009/11/cloud_computing_1.php

4. Seth Rosenblatt, "15 years of Download.com, the original app store," *CNET*, October 18, 2011. http://download.cnet.com/8301-2007_4 -20121351-12/15-years-of-download.com-the-original-app-store/

5. I had a chance to talk with Chase Norlin, who is the cofounder of ShareYourWorld.com. I asked him what the difference, if any, was between ShareYourWorld.com and YouTube and he told me, "It's exactly the same." He added, "It was the first YouTube. When you're first and you don't win, people forget. That's why many people don't know me and Tom started that, people only remember the guys who started YouTube, but it's the same service."

6. As it turns out, "there's nothing new under the sun" is a saying that comes from The Bible. Ecclesiastes 1:9, which says, "What has been will be again, what has been done will be done again; there is nothing new under the sun." Who knew?

7. Jim Yardley, "Vendorville," *The New York Times*, March 8, 1998, http://www.nytimes.com/1998/03/08/magazine/vendorville.html

8. Vance H. Trimble, *Sam Walton: The Inside Story of America's Richest Man*. (New York: Signet, 1991).

9. I asked my friends at Compete.com if they had thought about updating a study they did in 2006 that refuted some of Chris Anderson's "The Long Tail" theory when it came to what Web sites people were visiting and how much time they were spending with them. You can see what they found here: Jen Duguay, "The Long Tail Internet Myth: We Are Spending More Time on Top 10 Sites Than Ever," *Complete Pulse*. December 1, 2011. http://blog.compete.com/2011/12/01/the-long-tail-in ternet-myth-we-are-spending-more-time-on-top-10-sites-than-ever/. The results won't surprise you.

10. The Center for American Progress reportedly makes $25 million a year, so don't think for a second that they're a small operation that managed to sneak their way into the top ten most popular blogs. See Charlie Savage, "John Podesta, Shepherd of a Government in Exile," *The New York Times*. November 6, 2008. http://www.nytimes.com/2008/11/07/us/politics/07podesta.html?_r=1&ref=politics

11. Dan Lyons, technology editor of *Newsweek*, in conversation with the author. October 2011.

12. Facebook as the number one destination on the Web for Americans: Nielsen, *State of the Media: The Social Media Report*. Q3 2011. http://blog.nielsen.com/nielsenwire/social/

13. Facebook Steals: Farhad Manjoo, "Great Social Networks Steal," *Slate*, September 15, 2011. http://www.slate.com/articles/technology/technology/2011/09/great_social_networks_steal.html; Casey Chan, "Facebook Is Going to Add Instagram-style Photo Filters to their Facebook App," *Gizmodo*. August 24, 2011. http://gizmodo.com/5834135/facebook-is-going-to-add-instagram+style-photo-filters-to-their-facebook-app; Jason Kincaid, "Facebook Activates 'Like' Button: Friendfeed Tires of Sincere Flattery," *TechCrunch*, February 9, 2009. http://techcrunch.com/2009/02/09/facebook-activates-like-button-friendfeed-tires-of-sincere-flattery/; Dan Rowinski, "Facebook Releases Smart Friends List to Counter Google+ Circles," *ReadWriteWeb*, September 13, 2011. http://www.readwriteweb.com/archives/facebook_releases_smart_friend_lists_to_counter_go.php; Matthew Shaer, "With Subscribe Button, Facebook Steals a Page from the Twitter Playbook," *The Christian Science Monitor*. September 15, 2011. http://www.csmonitor.com/Innovation/Horizons/2011/0915/With-subscribe-button-Facebook-steals-a-page-from-the-Twitter-playbook; http://timelines.com/trademark; Jose Antonio Vargas, "The Face of Facebook," *The New Yorker*, September 20, 2010. http://www.new

yorker.com/reporting/2010/09/20/100920fa_fact_vargas
?currentPage=all

Go watch *The Social Network*. It's not accurate, but then again, nobody but the Winklevoss twins, their lawyers, Zuckerberg, and his lawyers, have seen all the evidence, because it was all sealed as part of the settlement. So how inaccurate it is is anyone's guess.

Aaron Greenspan also settled out of court with Facebook over a trademark dispute. Zuckerberg allegedly created material for house-SYSTEM at Harvard that ended up in Facebook when it launched. You can find the announcement about the out of court settlement here: http://www.insidefacebook.com/2009/05/22/facebook-announces-settlement-of-legal-dispute-with-another-former-Zuckerberg-classmate

You can also find a timeline created by Greenspan that documents the amount of time Zuckerberg spent using houseSYSTEM, their interactions, and things that Greenspan claims were borrowed and incorporated into Facebook here: http://www.thinkpress.com/authoritas/timeline.pdf;

Greenspan declined to comment for this book.

Tyler Winklevoss, one of the cofounders of HarvardConnection, in discussion with the author. October 2011.

For additional reading on Facebook's approach to user privacy, see: Liz Gannes, "The Apologizes of Zuckerberg: A Retrospective," *All Things D.* November 29, 2011. http://allthingsd.com/20111129/the-apologies-of-zuckerberg-a-retrospective/; For the record: I tried numerous times to speak with employees at Facebook, including Mark Zuckerberg. They did not reply to phone calls, e-mails, messages through Facebook, or (ironically) Google+.

14. Google's market share came under scrutiny by the Senate Judiciary Committee just as I was finishing this book. If you go here: http://judiciary.senate.gov/hearings/hearing.cfm?id=3d9031b47812de2592c3baeba64d93cb and click on "webcast," you can see former Google CEO Eric Schmidt point out that Google's share of the market is below the

threshold (80 percent) used to determine whether or not an organization has a monopoly.

15. Danny Sullivan, editor-in-chief of Search Engine Land, in discussion with the author, June 2011.

16. David Goldman, "Microsoft's plan to stop Bing's $1 billion bleeding," *CNN Money*, September 20, 2011. http://money.cnn.com/2011/09/20/technology/microsoft_bing/index.htm

17. Gabriel Weinberg, founder of DuckDuckGo, in discussion with the author, October 2011.

18. Now, you might be thinking, "People don't have to use Google, Facebook, or any of these other places. They have a choice." Unfortunately, that's wishful thinking. For further reading on the subject, I recommend *The Paradox Of Choice* and Sheena Iyengar's *The Art of Choosing*. See also: Alina Tugend, "Too Many Choices: A Problem That Can Paralyze," *The New York Times*, February 26, 2010. http://www.nytimes.com/2010/02/27/your-money/27shortcuts.html; and Steve Lohr, "The Default Choice, So Hard to Resist," *The New York Times*, October 15, 2011. http://www.nytimes.com/2011/10/16/technology/default-choices-are-hard-to-resist-online-or-not.html?pagewanted=all

19. Between May of 2009 to December 2009, in the heart of the Great Recession, the number of "social media marketers, gurus, ninjas, experts" and others exploded from 4,487 to 15,740 according to B. L. Ochman: http://www.whatsnextblog.com/2009/12/self-proclaimed_social_media_gurus_on_twitter_multiplying_like_rabbits/

20. Fox, Tricia. "Amy Winehouse's Untimely Death Is a Wake Up Call for Small Business Owners," *The Huffington Post*, July 24, 2011. http://www.huffingtonpost.com/tricia-fox/self-employed-risks_b_907921

.html. Those are direct quotes from Tricia Fox's Huffpo bio, which can be found here: http://www.huffingtonpost.com/tricia-fox. At the time of this writing, she's only done one other post besides the Amy Winehouse article. I reached out to Peter Goodman, business editor at The Huffington Post for comment on Tricia's post, but he declined to reply to calls and emails seeking comment.

21. Amazon is just as dominant as Google and Facebook, I just didn't mention them here because it's beyond the scope of this book: http://www.slideshare.net/faberNovel/amazoncom-the-hidden-empire

## Chapter 6

1. George Carlin, *Napalm and Silly Putty* (New York, NY: Hyperion, 2002).

2. Ibid.

3. Ibid.

4. Dylan Stableford, "Arianna Huffington: Go Ahead, Go on Strike—No One Will Notice," *Wrap*, March 3, 2011. http://thewrap.com/media/column-post/arianna-huffington-go-ahead-go-strike-no-one-will-notice-25230

5. Nate Silver, "The Economics of Blogging and The Huffington Post," *FiveThirtyEight*, February 12, 2011. http://fivethirtyeight.blogs.nytimes.com/2011/02/12/the-economics-of-blogging-and-the-huffington-post/

6. Ryan Lawler, "2 Out of 3 Youtube Videos Are Ignored," *NewTeeVee*, April 19, 2011. http://gigaom.com/video/youtube-long-tail-dead/; If you want further proof that nobody watches most of the stuff uploaded

to YouTube, see Google's $100 million effort to create original content exclusive to YouTube on: Amir Efrati, "YouTube Goes Professional," *The Wall Street Journal*, October 4, 2011. http://online.wsj.com/article/SB10001424052970204612504576609101775893100.html

7. Nicholas Carr, "Sharecropping the Long Tail," *Rough Type*, December 19, 2006. http://www.roughtype.com/archives/2006/12/sharecropping_t.php

8. Nicholas Carr, author of "The Shallows," in conversation with the author, September 2011.

9. I had an extensive conversation with James Erwin, author and screenwriter for "Rome Sweet Rome," concerning Carr's sharecropper model concept and his own Internet success story. James had a great counterpoint about Carr's sharecropper model that I wanted to share here: "A sharecropper in the real world is exhausted and angry by their work. They have few choices. They're trapped. Creating something like RSR [Rome Sweet Rome], however, is fun and invigorating—and that would have been just as true if I'd never made a dime. I know that everything I post on the Internet has a monetary value—it's just that the hassle of monetizing everything involves opportunity cost. It's not worth it to me. Same is true for a lot of other people."

10. Staff Reports, "A Note to Huffington Post High School Parents," *The Huffington Post*, October 14, 2011. http://www.huffingtonpost.com/2011/10/04/a-note-to-huffpost-high-s_n_969832.html

11. Jeff Bercovici, staff reporter at *Forbes*, in conversation with the author, October 2011.

12. Gautham Nagesh, "Facebook to Form Its Own PAC to Back Political Candidates," *The Hill*. September 26, 2011. http://thehill.com

/blogs/hillicon-valley/technology/183951-facebook-forming-own-pac
-to-back-candidates

13. Laurel Rosenhall, "Facebook Works to Make Friends at California's
Capitol," *The Sacramento Bee*. July 5, 2011. http://www.sacbee.com
/2011/07/05/3747370/facebook-works-to-make-friends.html

14. Addy Dugdale, "Former FTC Chair Timothy Muris to Steer Facebook Through Washington," *Fast Company*. May 10, 2010. http://www
.fastcompany.com/1643156/former-ftc-chair-timothy-muris-to-steer
-facebook-through-washington

15. Ryan Tate, "Facebook Just Played the Government," *Gawker*. November 29, 2011. http://gawker.com/5863493/facebook-just-played-the
-government. See also: http://www.ftc.gov/opa/2011/11/privatesettle
ment.ghtm

16. You can get updated information on how Facebook is spending its
money in Washington from the fantastic OpenSecrets.org: http://www
.opensecrets.org/lobby/clientsum.php?id=D000033563&year=2011

17. Emily Bazelon, "Why Facebook Is After Your Kids," *The New York
Times*. October 12, 2011. http://www.nytimes.com/2011/10/16/maga
zine/why-facebook-is-after-your-kids.html?_r=2

18. Nielsen, *State of the Media: The Social Media Report*. Q3 2011.
http://blog.nielsen.com/nielsenwire/social/

## Chapter 7

1. Christopher Mims, "Web 2.0 Will Die on October 1st, 2012,"
*Mims's Bits*, August 1, 2011. http://www.technologyreview.com/blog

/mimssbits/27049/; You can see the term "social media" take off as Web 2.0 declines here: http://www.google.com/insights/search/#q=social %20media%2CWeb%202.0&cmpt=q; I acknowledge these indicators aren't perfect, but remember: There are few better indicators out there to see what people are interested in than search. AOL's entire business model is built off this, as are all the other corporate blogs I told you about.

2. Darcy DiNucci, originator of the term *Web 2.0* (at least in a publication), in conversation with the author. October 2011.

3. Paul Graham, "Web 2.0," November 2005. http://www.paulgraham .com/web20.html

4. Ryan Singel, "Are You Ready for Web 2.0?" *Wired*, October 6, 2005. http://www.wired.com/science/discoveries/news/2005/10/69114

5. Paul Graham, "Web 2.0," November 2005. http://www.paulgraham .com/web20.html

6. Scott Laningham, "DeveloperWorks Interviews: Tim Berners-Lee," IBM DeveloperWorks. August 22, 2006. http://www.ibm.com/devel operworks/podcast/dwi/cm-int082206txt.html

7. Hamilton Nolan, Gawker.com editor, in conversation with the author, October 2011.

8. Drew Curtis, founder of Fark.com, in conversation with the author, November 2011.

9. Pew Research Center for the People & the Press. "Press Widely Criticized, But Trusted More than Other Information Sources," Pew Research Center, September 22, 2011. http://www.people-press.org/2011/09/22 /press-widely-criticized-but-trusted-more-than-other-institutions/

10. You can see Sir Tim Berners-Lee call Web 2.0 a "useful term" at 6:23 into this video: http://blip.tv/web-20-summit/web-2-0-summit-09-tim-berners-lee-and-tim-o-reilly-a-conversation-with-tim-berners-lee-2784292

11. Sir Tim Berners-Lee, the guy who invented the Web, in conversation with the author, August 2011.

12. Jimmy Wales, cofounder of Wikipedia, in discussion with the author, November 2011.

13. I'm paraphrasing Jeremiah Owyang who said, "I prefer the term 'Social Media' as I'm unaware of a better term to use. There are folks that dislike the term 'Social Media,' so this is a post asking those that don't like it to suggest a better term. If they can convince me, I'll change my vernacular." The comment came from: http://www.web-strategist.com/blog/2007/01/31/hate-the-term-social-media-help-come-up-with-a-better-term/

14. Staff Reports, "Jay Rosen on Journalism in the Internet Age," *The Browser*. July 24, 2011. http://thebrowser.com/interviews/jay-rosen-on-journalism-internet-age

15. Matthew Shechmeister, "Ghost Pages: A Wired.com Farewell To GeoCities," *Wired*. November 3, 2009. http://www.wired.com/rawfile/2009/11/geocities/all/1

16. To be clear, and this is a point also raised by Jeff Jarvis, if Rosen had said, "Prior to 1999 it was difficult to build and sustain an audience using the Web," I would have agreed. Although Jarvis speculates that's what Rosen was getting at, I don't know for sure if that was the case. I reached out to Rosen to see if that interpretation of his statement would be accurate, but he did not respond. Since I can't put words in Jay's mouth, I addressed the comments he had already made.

17. Staff Reports. "Yahoo! Buys GeoCities," *CNN Money*, January 28, 1999. "http://money.cnn.com/1999/01/28/technology/yahoo_a/

18. Milan, Mark. "GeoCities Time Has Expired, Yahoo Closing the Site Today," *The Los Angeles Times*. October 26, 2009. http://latimes blogs.latimes.com/technology/2009/10/geocities-closing.html

19. Ward Cunningham, "Wiki Wiki Origina," *Cunningham & Cunningham, Inc.* Date Unknown. http://c2.com/cgi/wiki?WikiWikiOrigin

20. Bryce Roberts, "Love or Hate Sean Parker," *Bryce Dot VC*. October 2011. http://bryce.vc/post/10634237662/love-or-hate-sean-parker-the -guy-has-been-at-the

21. Ibid.

22. The history of Napster is . . . convoluted at best. Plus, Sean Parker, as with all great self-promoters, has a tendency to exaggerate. Hey, it clearly worked; he's a billionaire, but it's hard to piece together who did what and had what role at the service. I attempted to interview both Parker and Fanning for this book to clear that up but was unsuccessful.

23. Ernesto at TorrentFreak.com pointed me to two different studies about Napster. One supported much of what I said here—that Napster's impact on sales is overstated. The second one documented how the people who were downloading wouldn't have bought the song before-hand, and after they downloaded it, were more likely to buy songs and albums from that band. Those studies are: *The Effects of Napster on Recorded Music Sales: Evidence from the Consumer Expedition Survey* (Stanford University): http://siepr.stanford.edu/publicationsprofile/379; *The Effect of File Sharing on Record Sales* (Harvard Business School and UNC Chapel Hill) http://www.unc.edu/~cigar/papers/FileSharing_June2005 _final.pdf

24. Ben Popper, "Mike Arrington Goes Nuclear: Says NY Times Is Conflicted Tech Investor via True Ventures," *Beta Beat*. September 12, 2011. http://www.betabeat.com/2011/09/12/mike-arrington-goes-nuclear-says-ny-times-is-conflicted-tech-investor-via-true-ventures/

25. Habib Kairouz, "Buckle up: Traditional TV Is in for a Heck of a Ride," *GigaOm*, September 2011. http://gigaom.com/video/buckle-up-traditional-tv-is-in-for-a-heck-of-a-ride/

26. A lot of the stuff about the media was omitted from this book because it was way too off topic for what is, ultimately, a marketing book. However there's one piece of a discussion I had with Dr. Robert Thompson at Syracuse University's S. I. Newhouse School of Public Communications that I think is worth sharing here concerning technology's "disruption" of the news business. This is what Dr. Thompson said: "The most fatal thing [the media] did was jump in without a plan, and this started a long time ago before social media, to the detriment of important civic organizations. When the online stuff exploded media, newspapers, universities, they all worried they weren't on top of things or of being thought of as the 'Square Old Media' and having people say that all of these institutions are 'dinosaurs.'

"I remember when I could first go online to read *The New York Times*, it was difficult for me to get, up here in Syracuse, and when that happened I stopped buying it. But that's a great example of jumping in without a plan. My dad was a plumber, and how they put everything online for free and in a linkable way was like if he had gone and put water heaters in people's homes for free.

"It gave everyone a sense of entitlement. Now finally they're trying to put up firewalls and people scream and carry on about it, but the idea of jumping in without a viable plan, even before social media, has resulted in chaos, but if they hadn't put their stuff online in linkable ways, none of this stuff would have happened.

"And in that chaos you get stuff like CNN saying on the air 'Let's see what the blogs and social media have to say.' That's like a surgeon stopping surgery half way and walking into the waiting room to ask the people there what they think."

## Chapter 8

1. John D. Sutter, "Ashton Kutcher Challenges CNN to Twitter Popularity Contest," CNN. April 15, 2009. http://articles.cnn.com/2009 -04-15/tech/ashton.cnn.twitter.battle_1_cnn-twitter-account-follow ers?_s=PM:TECH

2. Jack Neff, "Why More of Your Facebook Fans are Seeing Fewer of Your Messages," *AdAge*, October 31, 2011. http://adage.com/article /digital/reach-beats-frequency-facebook-s-layout/230718/

3. Sheila Shayon, "The Justin Bieber Phenomenon: Social Media On Steroids," The Huffington Post, March 25, 2010. http://www.huffing-tonpost.com/sheila-shayon/the-justin-bieber-phenome_b_513106 .html

4. Sheila Shaylon is the president of Third Eye Media, an "end-to-end multimedia production, Web design, and software development group." Ironically, the company also claims it was created to, "excise the hype and bulk that is unneeded to communicate simply and powerfully."

5. Liz Shannon Miller pointed me to this link that explains why the YouTube system for counting views is so secretive: http://www.google .com/support/forum/p/youtube/thread?tid=6abc6fdf32d2b278& hl=en

6. Erik Schonfeld, "ComScore: YouTube Now 25 Percent of All Google Searches," *TechCrunch*, December 18, 2008. http://techcrunch.com/

2008/12/18/comscore-youtube-now-25-percent-of-all-google-searches/
?rss

7.Felicia Williams, former entertainment content manager at YouTube, in discussion with the author, October 2011.

8. Evan Gregory, of The Gregory Brothers, in conversation with the author, November 2011.

9. Ibid.

10. There is something to be said for "first mover advantage," which is a hideous marketing term often used to describe the benefit of being some-where before your competitors are. Although there's some truth to it, it's impossible to know what platform is going to take off and which ones won't. As Gary Vaynerchuk pointed out to me, for every platform he thought was going to take off like Twitter, there was another like Plurk that didn't. I don't think it's in anyone's best interest to play the guessing game of which start-up is going to take off when. And although it's true that a lot of the people with huge view counts on YouTube got in early and were smart enough to network with each other, that doesn't mean you can replicate that success, given the right resources, timing, and other consid-erations. First mover advantage tends to stick more when you're talking about smaller or more specific markets.

11. There was a great thread on Quora that broke down how the "Double Rainbow" video became a "meme." You can check that out here: http://www.quora.com/Double-Rainbows/Why-is-the-Double-Rainbow-video-funny

12. Staff Reports, "Cashing In: Video Partners Split Ad Revenue with YouTube, Creating Big Payday for the Once-Obscure," *The Wall Street Journal*, February 2012, http://www.onwsj.com/zaJ50R

13. Jesus Diaz, "Justin Bieber Has Dedicated Servers at Twitter," *Gizmodo*, September 7, 2010. http://gizmodo.com/5632095/justin-bieber-has-dedicated-servers-at-twitter

14. Liz Shannon Miller, coeditor of NewTeeVee, in discussion with the author, September 2011.

15. Nielsen, *State Of The Media: The Social Media Report*, Q3 2011. http://blog.nielsen.com/nielsenwire/social/

16. Ben Steinbauer, *Winnebago Man*, directed by Ben Steinbauer (2009: San Fransisco: Bear Media, 2009.), DVD.

17. Michael D. Ayers, "CBS to Develop Series Based on Popular Twitter Account," AOL TV. November 10, 2009. http://www.aoltv.com/2009/11/10/cbs-to-develop-series-based-on-popular-twitter-account/

18. Eric Becker, creator of the Fake Michael Bay Twitter account, in conversation with the author, April 2011.

19. Kayla Webley, "Halpern on Twitter and 'Sh*t My Dad Says,'" *Time* magazine. May 21, 2010. http://www.time.com/time/arts/article/0,8599,1990838,00.html

20. Rob Corddry, actor and comedian, in conversation with the author, November 2011.

21. There is a comic by a Tunisian redditor pointing out the difference the media made in the coverage of the Tunisian uprising on reddit compared to the coverage about the Egyptian uprising. If you're not totally sold on the effects the media and celebrities have on things they plug on the Web, you can find that comic at: http://i.imgur.com/5lxNp.jpg

22. Justin Halpern, creator of Shit My Dad Says, in conversation with the author, April 2011.

23. Ibid.

## Chapter 9

1. Seth Godin, *All Marketers Are Liars: The Power of Telling Authentic Stories in a Low-Trust World* (Portfolio Hardcover: New York, NY, 2005).

2. Dan Lyons, "All of life has been utterly, profoundly changed thanks to Facebook's new features, and nothing will ever be the same, and all I can do is sit here and weep at the beauty and magic that Mark Zuckerberg has brought to this world," *Real Dan Lyons*, September 23, 2011. http://www.realdanlyons.com/blog/2011/09/23/all-of-life-has-been-utterly-profoundly-changed-thanks-to-facebooks-new-changes-and-nothing-will-ever-be-the-same-and-all-i-can-do-is-sit-here-and-weep-at-the-beauty-and-magic-that-mark-zuckerberg/

3. I don't get into it too much in this book, but in discussions of the Arab Spring and Occupy Wall Street you can see the Cyber Hipsters utilizing Maslow's hammer to describe these events and the role technology had in making those movements happen. For more in-depth discussion of the Cyber Hipsters and their narrow-minded world view, I recommend you read *The Net Delusion* by Evgeny Morozov. Just replace "Iran" with "Egypt" and you will see what I mean.

4. Shirky can be seen describing the fight against SOPA as a "leaderless movement" at http://www.YouTube.com/wathc?V=GsxvGl5hJgE

5. Kalle Lasn, in conversation with the author, February 2011.

6. Farhad Manjoo, "Long Tails and Big Heads," *Slate*, July 14, 2008. http://www.slate.com/articles/technology/2008/07/long-tails_and_big_heads.html.

7. For more on writers coming out of Harvard (potentially) getting ahead of other writers in the television field, see: http://www.jerriblank.com/odonnell.html and Tina Fey, "Lessons from Late Night," *The New Yorker*. March 14, 2011. http://www.newyorker.com/reporting/2011/03/14/110314fa_fact_fey; There's also some discussion of it in *The Simpsons: An Uncensored, Unauthorized, History* by John Ortved.

8. There is an often cited statistic from a July 2006 edition of *Publishers Weekly* that states most books in America don't sell more than five hundred copies, and far fewer sell more than a thousand.

9. Marina Krakovsky, "Readers Tap Best-Seller List for New Authors," *Stanford Business Magazine*. February 2005. http://www.gsb.stanford.edu/news/bmag/sbsm0502/research_sorensen_consumers.shtml

10. BanuRekha Mahadevan, client relations consultant of Brickwork India, in conversation with the author, March 2011.

11. John Dvorak, "Are Amazon Reviews Corrupt?" *PC Magazine*, June 28, 2011. http://www.pcmag.com/article2/0,2817,2387749,00.asp#fbid=bNY7CplYOPe

12. Richard Cleland, assistant director of the division of advertising practices at the FTC, in conversation with the author, August 2011. See also: David Streifeld, "For $2 a Star, an Online Retailer Gets 5 Star Product Reviews," *The New York Times*, January 26, 2012. http://www.nytimes.com/2012/01/27/technology/for-2-a-star-a-retailer-gets-5-star-reviews.html

## Chapter 10

1. Brian Solis, "The Social Media Manifesto," *Brian Solis*, June 11, 2007. http://www.briansolis.com/2007/06/future-of-communications-manifesto-for/. Solis has since gone on to claim he is not a "social media" expert.

2. You can see the pricing for the 2010 Web 2.0 Summit here: http://www.web2summit.com/web2010/public/content/pricing. The price for the Mashable Connect 2012 can be found here: http://mashableconnect2012-sidebar.eventbrite.com.

3. Malcom Gladwell, *The Tipping Point* (Little, Brown and Company: New York, 2000).

4. If you didn't get the Long Island nightclub reference, see: Staff Reports, "Highlights of Interviews With Rosie O'Donnell," CNN. March 16, 2002. http://transcripts.cnn.com/TRANSCRIPTS/0203/16/lklw.00.html

5. You can see the box office data for *Scott Pilgrim vs. The World* here: http://www.the-numbers.com/movies/2010/SPILG.php and http://www.the-numbers.com/movies/2009/WATCH.php. *Watchmen* wound up making its money back in the long run, which is sad because it's not a good film. Read the graphic novel instead.

6. Tucker Max, in conversation with the author, March 15, 2011.

7. Nick Douglas, "Twitter blows up at SXSW conference," *Gawker*, March 12, 2007, http://gawker.com/tech/next-big-thing/twitter-blows-up-at-sxsw-conference-243634.php

8. Daniel Terdiman, "To Twitter or Dodgeball at SXSW?" *CNET*, March 10, 2007, http://news.cnet.com/8301-17939_109-9696264-2.html

9. Nielsen, "Twitter's Tweet Smell of Success," *nielsenwire*. March 18, 2009. http://blog.nielsen.com/nielsenwire/online_mobile/twitters-tweet-smell-of-success/

10. This information comes from a report put out by the Pew Internet & American Life Project on June 1, 2011. It can be accessed at: http://www.pewinternet.org/Reports/2011/Twitter-Update-2011.aspx

11. Mona Zhang, "Growth of Twitter Fueled by Media Coverage," *10,000 Words*, December 22, 2011. http://www.mediabistro.com/10000words/growth-of-twitter-fueled-by-media-coverage-mit-study-b9429

12. You can see the Twitter announcement here: https://twitter.com/#!/twitterglobalpr/status/108285017792331776

13. Lesley Goldberg, "MTV's Video Music Awards Scores Largest Audience Ever," *Hollywood Reporter*, http://www.hollywoodreporter.com/live-feed/mtvs-video-music-awards-scores-228952

14. Gary drives me crazy sometimes. He's a smart guy and good at what he does, but occasionally he'll say stuff that I don't think makes much sense. You can watch that particular Vaynerchuk video here: http://www.youtube.com/watch?v=u57GQZT3mVI.

15. The 2010 VMAs had 11.4 million viewers and the 2011 VMAs had 12.4 million viewers. You can see the ratings breakdown on the Wikipedia page here: http://en.wikipedia.org/wiki/MTV_Video_Music_Award#cite_note-hitsdailydouble.com-108

16. Nowhere in *any* write-up about how platforms like Twitter are "fueling" ratings growth for live television will you hear mentioned how live television has been doing well since the economy fell apart.

17. Jennifer Van Grove, "Twitter CEO Dick Costolo: 2012 Is Going to Be the Twitter Election," January 30, 2102. http://wwwventurebeat .com/2012/01/30/dick-costolo-twitter-media

18. Buddy Roemer, in conversation with the author, February 2012.

19. All the information on Dr. Milgram and his experiment came from the articles cited in the footnotes of his Wikipedia page, Dr. Watt's book *Everything Is Obvious, Once You Know the Answer,* and interviewing Dr. Watts and Dr. Kleinfeld. See also: Monica Hesse, "Many Media Types Live in the Land of Twitter, but Most Regular People Don't," *All Twitter,* May 17, 2011. http://www.washingtonpost.com/lifestyle/style/many -media-types-live-in-the-land-of-twitter-but-most-regular-people -don't/2011/09/01/s1aARFavcw_stork.html

20. Duncan J. Watts, *Everything Is Obvious, Once You Know the Answer* (New York, NY: Crown Business. 2011.)

21. Dr. Judith Kleinfeld, University Of Alaska-Fair Banks professor, in conversation with the author, July 2011.

22. Dr. Duncan J. Watts, author of *Everything Is Obvious, Once You Know the Answer,* in conversation with the author, August 2011.

23. I'm not going to lie, I enjoy those TED videos as much as the next person, but there's a lot that former TechCrunch writer, Sara Lacy, has documented that concerns me about the conference. This particular quote from the dis-invited TED attendee you can access at: http://tech crunch.com/2011/02/27/the-haves-and-have-nots-the-true-story-of- a-reader-suddenly-de-invited-from-ted/?utm_source=feedburner&utm _medium=feed&utm_campaign=Feed%3A+ Techcrunch+(TechCrunch)

## Chapter 11

1. Elizabeth Shaw, Jennifer Wise, David Truog, and Sarah Takvorian, "Case Study: USA Network Wins Over Fans Through Gamification," *Forrester Research*, September 28, 2011. http://www.forrester.com/rb /Research/case_study_usa_network_wins_over_fans/q/id/60285/t/2

2. Jeremiah Owyang, Andrew Jones, Christine Tran, and Andrew Nguyen, "Social Business Readiness: How Advanced Companies Prepare Internally," *Altimeter Group*, August 31, 2011. http://www.altim etergroup.com/2011/08/research-report-be-prepared-by-climbing-the -social-business-hierarchy-of-needs.html

3. Ibid.

4. You can find the related graph here: http://www.flickr.com/photos/ jeremiah_owyang/6098016293/

5. Ibid.

6. Marc Rees, "25 000 &euro$ d'indemnités pour un exemple supprimé de Wikipedia," *PC Inpact*, July 4, 2011. http://www.pcinpact.com /actu/news/64468-rentabiliweb-hi-media-micropaiement-wikipedia .htm

7. Sarah Perez, "Steve Jobs Had No Heart Attack . . . And Citizen Journalism Just Failed," *ReadWriteWeb*, October 3, 2008. http://www .readwriteweb.com/archives/steve_jobs_had_no_heart_attack_citi zen_journalism_failed.php

8. This wouldn't be the last time an outside party did damage to Apple's stock due to a lack of oversight from a major media company. See: Marc Hustvedt, "What's Trending Forges on After Split from CBS," *Tubefil-*

*ter News*. September 13, 2011.http://news.tubefilter.tv/2011/09/13/
whats-trending-cbs/

9. Alex Alvarez, "Stephen Colbert on CNN iReporters: 'This Bold Move
Will Help You Get Rid of Your Remaining Viewers,'" November 29,
2011. http://www.mediaite.com/tv/stephen-colbert-on-cnn-ireporters
-this-bold-move-will-help-you-get-rid-of-your-remaining-viewers/

10. Staff Reports, "GoDaddy CEO's Graphic Elephant Hunt Video
Sends His Clients Flocking to Competitors, and Helps Raise $20,000
for Elephant Charity," *The Daily Mail*, April 8 2011, http://www.daily
mail.co.uk/news/article-1374679/GoDaddy-CEO-Bob-Parsons-ele-
phant-shooting-video-pays-Namecheap-Save-Elephants.html

11. Joshua Stearns, the associate program director at FreePress.net, described the effects of the 1996 Telecommunications Act on the media
landscape as follows: "The 1996 Telecommunications Act has had a pro-
found impact on the shape of American media. While it was supposed to
usher in the age of the Internet, it also unleashed a wave of new media
consolidation that has left America with less local journalism and fewer
diverse voices. You used to be able to travel around the country and hear
local music being played, hear local issues being debated, and hear the
viewpoints of local people being given a voice. But now, thanks to policies
like the 1996 Telecom Act and decisions at the Federal Communications
Commission since, everything sounds the same. Playlists get programmed
out of state and pumped into local communities, news (where there is any
at all) is full of celebrity gossip and sensationalism, and local DJs are becoming an endangered species".

## Chapter 12

1. Stephen J. Dubner, Steven D. Levitt, *Freakonomics: A Rogue Economist Explores the Hidden Side of Everything* (New York: William Morrow. 2005.)

2. You can find the landing page for Chris's seminar here: http://www .humanbusinessworks.com/landing/googleplusbiz

3. Chris makes that statement at the start of his YouTube video.

4. David Sarno, "Google+ Continues Battle with Fading User Interest, Data Says," *The Los Angeles Times*, November 17, 2011. http://latimes blogs.latimes.com/technology/2011/11/google-plus-traffic.html

5. Chris Brogan, "A Day in the Life," *Chris Brogan*, July 19, 2011. http:// www.chrisbrogan.com/a-day-in-the-life-2/

6. The exact line is, "Do NOT miss this opportunity to learn Google+ from the guy who made Twitter a business staple back in 2006, and who will do the same for business in 2011." This can be found on the landing page cited at http://www.humanbusinessworks.com/landing/google plusbiz.

7. Chris signed up for Twitter on October 24, 2006. You can find out when anyone signed up for the service here: http://www.whendidyou jointwitter.com/

8. Matt McGee, "Google Removes Mashable, Sesame Street and Other Prominent Accounts from Google Plus," *Search Engine Land*. July 21, 2011. http://searchengineland.com/google-removes-mashable-sesame -street-other-prominent-accounts-from-google-plus-86788

9. Larry Dignan, "Ford aims to use Google's Prediction API to bolster analytics," *ZDNET,* May 10, 2011. http://www.zdnet.com/blog/btl/ford-aims-to-use-googles-prediction-api-to-bolster-analytics/48493

10. Jakob Nielsen, "Participation Inequality: Encouraging More Users to Contribute," *Useit.* October 9, 2006. http://www.useit.com/alertbox/participation_inequality.html. See also: http://www.useit.com/alertbox/9709b.html. I spoke with Dr. Nielsen and asked him: (1) If he still stands by this post in 2011 and (2) Is it fair to say that the "community" may represent a minority that doesn't accurately make up the rest of someone's customers / audience? His responses were: (1) Yes. (2) Definitely.

11. Lizz Winstead, cocreator of *The Daily Show*, in conversation with the author, September 2011.

12. Nate Hirst, global marketing analyst at Blendtec, in conversation with the author, September 2011.

13. Kristen Nicole, "Will It Blend Videos Boost Sales 5X," *Mashable*, September 27, 2007. http://mashable.com/2007/09/27/blendtec-sales/

14. Chris Crocker did not reply to requests seeking comment.

15. Felicia Williams, former entertainment content manager at YouTube, in conversation with the author, September 2011. Felicia made it a point to state that her views on this particular item were "based on my opinion, memory, and observations as a professional in video at the time and does not reflect YouTube as a company or reveal any insider info."

16. Joshua Davis, "The Secret World of Lonely Girl," *Wired*, December 2006, http://www.wired.com/wired/archive/14.12/lonelygirl.html

17. Nate Hirst, Global Marketing Analyst at Blendtec, in conversation with the author, September 2011.

18. Ev Williams, former CEO of Twitter, in conversation with the author, October 2011.

19. Dave Delaney, "Communication 2.0—Zappos: A Social Media Success Story. Interview with Tony Hsieh," *Dave Delaney*, July 9, 2008. http://www.davemadethat.com/2008/07/09/communication-20-zappos-a-social-media-success-story-interview-with-tony-hsieh/

20. Tony Hsieh, CEO of Zappos, in conversation with the author, September 2011.

21. Claire Cain Miller, "Dell Says It Has Earned $3 Million from Twitter," *The New York Times*, June 23. 12, 2009. http://bits.blogs.nytimes.com/2009/06/12/dell-has-earned-3-million-from-twitter/

22. Michael Ian Black, actor and comedian, in conversation with the author, November 2011.

23. Stefanie N., "@DellOutlet Surpasses $2 Million on Twitter," *Direct 2Dell*, June 11, 2009. http://en.community.dell.com/dell-blogs/direct2dell/b/direct2dell/archive/2009/06/11/delloutlet-surpasses-2-million-on-twitter.aspx

24. Dean McBeth, former senior digital strategist at Wieden + Kennedy, in conversation with the author, October 2011.

25. The numbers speak for themselves. Go to the Old Spice YouTube page and look at the Old Spice Internet Response videos with the highest views. They're all celebrities: http://www.youtube.com/user/OldSpice#g/c/484F058C3EAF7FA6

26. David Griner, "Hey Old Spice haters, sales are up 107%," *ADWeek*. July 27, 2010. http://www.adweek.com/adfreak/hey-old-spice-haters -sales-are-107-12422

27. Dean McBeth, former senior digital strategist at Wieden + Kennedy, in conversation with the author, October 2011.

28. Megan O'Neill, "Cisco Fails with Old Spice Copycat Campaign," *Social Times*, July 28, 2010. http://socialtimes.com/cisco-old-spice-cam paign_b18558

29. Dean McBeth, former senior digital strategist at Wieden + Kennedy, in conversation with the author, October 2011.

## Chapter 13

1. You have to be careful with infographics. They're (almost always) advertising disguised as content. That said, from personal experience I can vouch for the numbers they suggest it costs to run a social media campaign: http://www.focus.com/images/view/58313/

2. Stu Woo, "Facebook Won't Become E-Commerce Force, Analyst Says," *The Wall Street Journal*, April 7, 2011. http://blogs.wsj.com/dig its/2011/04/07/facebook-wont-become-e-commerce-force-analyst -says/

3. And not to put too fine a point on it, in their S-1 IPO Filing, Facebook states, "We generate a substantial majority of our revenue from advertising. The loss of advertisers, or a reduction in spending by advertisers with Facebook can seriously harm our business." Remember: Analysts state the obvious, so when they're saying stuff like what's in *The Wall Street Journal* article? It's worth taking notice. See Kit R. Roane, "Facebook:

Where Marketing Efforts Go to Die?" *Fortune*, April 6, 2011. http://tech
.fortune.cnn.com/2011/04/06/facebook-where-marketing-efforts-go-to
-die/. New Stakt Reports. "Most Consumers Still Don't Talk About
Brands on Social Sites," *eMarketer*, January 10, 2012, http://www.emar
keter.com/Article.aspx?R=1008773. Locke, Laura. "Facebook global revenue expected to hit 4.27B," *CNET*, September 20, 2011. http://news
.cnet.com/8301-1023_3-20109007-93/facebook-global-revenue-expected
-to-hit-$4.27b/. Sarah Needleman, "Facebook 'Likes' Small Business,"
*The Wall Street Journal*, September 26, 2011. http://online.wsj.com/arti
cle/SB10001424053111903791504576589353419786240.html

4. Shayndi Roice. "Is Facebook Ready for the Big Time?" *The Wall Street
Journal*, http://www.online.wsj.com/article/SB1000142405297.0204542
405240457715713178985408.html. This information came from 10
Facts About Consumer Behavior On Facebook: http://www.socialquick
starter.com/content/10310_facts_about_consumer_behavior_on_face
book. See Jeff Widman, "How Long Does a Status Update Stay in the
Facebook Newsfeed," *PageLever*, October 7, 2011. http://pagelever.com
/long-status-update-stay-facebook-newsfeed/. Brian Carter, "Shocker:
3% to 7.5% Of Fans See Your Page's Posts," *All Facebook*, June 21, 2011.
http://www.allfacebook.com/shocker-3-to-7-5-of-fans-see-your-pages
-posts-2011-06?utm_source=feedburner&utm_medium=feed&utm
_campaign=Feed%3A+allfacebook+%28Facebook+Blog%29

5. Matthew Creamer, "Study: Only 1% of Facebook 'Fans' Engage with
Brands," *AdAge*, January 27, 2011. http://www.adage.com/article/digi
tal/study-of-facebook-fans-engage-with-brands-23235. Those stats
about half of Facebook's users logging in once a day were accurate at the
time of this writing and came right from Facebook's official statistics
page. You can get the latest statistics about the service and its usage on
the same page: https://www.facebook.com/press/info.php?statistics.
See Robin Goad, "1 Facebook fan = 20 additional visits to your web-

site," *Experian Hitwise*, June 23, 2011. http://weblogs.hitwise.com
/robin-goad/2011/06/1_facebook_fan_20_additional_v.html. Josh
Constine, "Popular Facebook Pages Have Fewer Unique Page Views
Per Fan, Most Engagement Is in the News Feed," *Inside Facebook*, June
22, 2011. http://www.insidefacebook.com/2011/06/22/unique-page
-views/?utm_source=feedburner&utm_medium=feed&utm
_campaign=Feed%3A+InsideFacebook+%28Inside+Facebook%29.
Patricio Robles, "Facebook Pages Deliver Paltry CTRs: Report," *EConsultancy*, November 16, 2011. http://econsultancy.com/us/blog/8283
-facebook-pages-deliver-paltry-ctrs-report

6. Roberta Rosenberg, president of MGP Direct, Inc., in discussion
with the author, June 2011.

7. Jennifer Preston, "Pepsi Bets on Local Grants, Not the Super Bowl,"
*The New York Times*, January 30, 2011. http://www.nytimes.com/2011
/01/31/business/media/31pepsi.html?_r=2

8. Mike Esterl, "Diet Coke Wins Battle in Cola Wars," *Yahoo! Finance*,
March 17, 2011. http://finance.yahoo.com/family-home/article/112372/
diet-coke-wins-battle-in-cola-wars

9. Staff Reports. "PepsiCo Seeing Success with Pepsi Refresh Project,"
*Beverage World*, December 16, 2010. http://www.beverageworld.com
/index.php?option=com_content&view=article&id=38699:pepsico
-seeing-success-with-pepsi-refresh-project&catid=3:daily-headlines&
Itemid=173

10. JetBlue made it a point to say the answers to the questions I sent
them came from numerous parties within the marketing department,
so I can't pinpoint who exactly said what in that interview. The interview was conducted in September 2011.

11. That's taken word for word from the case study Facebook released, which you can find here: http://ads.ak.facebook.com/ads/Faceboo kAds/Kia_CaseStudy.pdf

12. Jennifer Moire, "How Kia Captured Coolness on Facebook," *All Facebook*, April 22, 2011. http://www.allfacebook.com/how-kia-cap tured-coolness-on-facebook-2011-04

13. With "social media" the rich get richer. You can see further proof of this by looking at what companies had the most shared articles on the service: CNN, Yahoo!, The Washington Post, The New York Times, and The Huffington Post. These stories, as pointed out by TechCrunch and other outlets, are almost all about parenting, which further supports the theory that Facebook is for family, not marketing. You can see the list of 2011's most shared stories here: https://www.facebook.com/note.php?note_id=283221585046671. There's plenty more about Facebook that can be found at http://www.delicious .com/bjmendelson

## Chapter 14

1. Chris Brogan, "I'm Not Selling to You," *Chris Brogan*, July 19, 2011. http://www.chrisbrogan.com/im-not-selling-to-you/

2. You can watch that video here. O'Reilly's comments on Keen's book come at 38:12 http://www.youtube.com/watch?v=WMSinyx_Ab0

3. Lawrence Lessig, "Keen's 'The Cult of the Amateur': Brilliant!" *Lessig 2.0.* May 31, 2007. http://www.lessig.org/blog/2007/05/keens_the _cult_of_the_amateur.html

4. Ibid.

5. Matthew Ingram, "Blaming the Tools: Britain Proposes a Social Media Ban," *GigaOm*, August 11, 2011. http://gigaom.com/2011/08/11/blaming-the-tools-britain-proposes-a-social-media-ban/

6. Jeff Jarvis, "Dinosaur Roar," *Buzzmachine*, April 21, 2005. http://www.buzzmachine.com/archives/2005_04_21.html

7. Jeff Jarvis, "Your Advice: Should I Debate?" *Buzzmachine*, May 10, 2007. http://www.buzzmachine.com/2007/05/10/your-advice-should-i-debate/

8. Malcom Gladwell, "Does Egypt Need Twitter?" *The New Yorker*, February 2, 2011. http://www.newyorker.com/online/blogs/newsdesk/2011/02/does-egypt-need-twitter.html

9. Malcolm Gladwell, "Small Change: Why the Revolution Will Not Be Tweeted," *The New Yorker*. October 4, 2010. http://www.newyorker.com/reporting/2010/10/04/101004fa_fact_gladwell

10. Evgeny Morozov, *The Net Delusion: The Dark Side of Internet Freedom* (Jackson, Tennessee: PublicAffairs, 2011).

11. Liz Gannes, "Twitter Founders: Gladwell Got It Wrong," *GigaOM*, October 11, 2010. http://gigaom.com/2010/10/11/twitter-founders-gladwell-got-it-wrong/

12. Chris Dixon, "What Malcom Gladwell Doesn't Get About Twitter," *The Faster Times*, October 24, 2010. http://www.thefastertimes.com/startups/2010/10/24/what-malcom-gladwell-doesnt-get-about-twitter/

13. You can watch the Chewbacca Defense on the South Park Studios Web site here: http://www.southparkstudios.com/clips/103454/the-chewbacca-defense

14. Biz Stone, "Exclusive: Biz Stone on Twitter and Activism," *The Atlantic*, October 19, 2010. http://www.theatlantic.com/technology/archive/2010/10/exclusive-biz-stone-on-twitter-and-activism/64772/

15. You can see the complete list of sites banned in China at http://en.wikipedia.org/wiki/list-of-websites-blocked-in-the-peoples-republic-of-china

16. Ryan Tate, "Tech's Most Useless Bigshot," *Gawker*, August 26, 2011. http://www.gawker.com/5834546/techs-most-useless-bigshot

17. Staff Reports. "Tweets Still Must Flow," *Twitter Blog*, January 26, 2012. http://blog.twitter.com/2012/01/30/tweets-still-must-flow

18. Evgeny Morozov, "The Internet Intellectual". *The New Republic*. October 12th, 2011. http://www.tnr.com/print/article/books/magazine/96116/the-internet-intellectual

19. I have a long list of shitty stuff Mashable and Pete Cashmore have done here: http://bjmendelson.com/2011/09/27/the-problem-with-my-friends-at-mashablecom/

## Chapter 15

1. Michael D'Antonio, *The True Story of Walter O'Malley, Baseball's Most Controversial Owner and the Dodgers of Brooklyn and Los Angeles,* (New York: Riverhead. 2009).

2. Fake It Until You Make It: Dan Schawbel, "The Real Role of Social Media," *Forbes*, September 26, 2011. http//www.forbes.com/sites/danschawbel/2011/09/26/the-real-role-of-social-meida/ and Mitch Joel,

"Fake It Until You Make It," *Six Pixels of Separation*, January 11, 2011. http://www.twistimage.com/glob/archives/fake-it-until-you-make-it

3. Harry G. Frankfurt, author of *On Bullshit*, in conversation with the author, October 2011.

4. Harry G. Frankfurt, *On Bullshit*, Princeton, New Jersey: Princeton University Press, 2005.

## Chapter 16

1. Ashley Lutz, "GameStop to JCPenney Shut Facebook Stores: Retail," *Bloomberg*, February 22, 2012. http://www.bloomberg.com/news/2012-02-17/e-commerce-trips-as-gap-to-penny-shut-facebook-stores-retail.htm

2. The numbers about the usage of foursquare came from Pew: http://pewinternet.org/Reports/2011/Location/Overview.aspx

3. Anytime you see me mention demographics and ages of people using a service, I got my information from: http://blog.nielsen.com/nielsenwire/social/

4. Celeste Atlus, "Journalists: We Love Twitter," *PRNewser*, November 18, 2011. http://www.mediabistro.com/prnewser/journalists-we-love-twitter_b30389

5. Tron Guy in conversation with the author, June 2011. Tron Guy, like everyone else I mentioned in this book who became famous (or at least, Internet Famous) took off because of the backing of powerful communities like Slashdot and Fark, two sites that are still going

strong today, but you almost never hear about because they're not the "hip" thing anymore.

6. Laura Hudson, "Scott Adams Poses as His Own Fan on Message Boards to Defend Himself," *ComicsAlliance*, April 20, 2011. http://www.comicsalliance.com/2011/04/20/scott-adams-plannedchaos-sockpuppet/. Disclosure: Up until AOL axed their freelancers, I used to contribute to ComicsAlliance.

7. George Johnson, "New Web Project," *Old Fashioned Patriot*, October 27, 2003. http://oldfashionedpatriot.blogspot.com/2003_10_01_old fashionedpatriot_archive.html#106727416975886151. See also: Noam Cohen, "Google Halts 'Miserable Failure' Link to President Bush," *The New York Times*, January 29, 2007; http://www.nytimes.com/2007/01/29/technology/29google.html; and Tom McNichol, "Your Message Here," *The New York Times*, January 22, 2004. http://www.nytimes.com/2004/01/22/technology/circuits/22goog.html?ex=1390194000&en=90e67992909e0ad4&ei=5007&partner=USERLAND

8. I know I said it earlier, but it's worth repeating: If you're waiting for the FTC or Google to do something proactive here, you're going to be dead before it happens.

## Chapter 17

1. You can read the first six chapters of *Dracula and Kittens* here: http://www.draculaandkittens.com

2. You can see the "Digital Dale Carnegie" reference on "social media" marketer Erik Qualman's about page: http://www.socialnomics.net/about-erik-qualman/

3. The full text of Roosevelt's speech can be found here: http://pub licpolicy.pepperdine.edu/faculty-research/new-deal/roosevelt -speeches/fr052232.htm

4. Evan White, chief marketing officer at Viddy, in conversation with the author, September 2011.

5. Ibid.

6. I called the colonel to confirm if he remembers saying that. He doesn't, but he said "I sure think it."

7. Jacquie Jordan, former television producer and author of *Get On TV!*, in conversation with the author, October 2011.

8. Larry Tye, *The Father of Spin: Edward L. Bernays and the Birth of Public Relations* (New York: Henry Holt and Company, 1998).

9. I don't like to plug things, but IMDB Pro was an excellent resource for this book, and for doing the things Jacquie talked about. You have to be careful as some of the information is not up to date (I had some weird conversations with former agents and managers of people like Jon Stewart because of this), but overall it's very good for finding the right people.

10. Okay. One more plug: If you're looking for a publicist, give my friend Jill Falcone Vedric a try. Her email is: jillvedric@gmail.com and her phone number is 516-317-2005. I don't do press and public relations, so when someone has contacted me to do it for them, I refer them to Jill. None of them have been disappointed.

11. Josh Kaufman, *The Personal MBA* (New York, NY: Portfolio. 2010).

12. It's important to draw a distinction between people who are creating and developing products and those talking about things like the Internet in a general sense. For the people reading this book, the ones who have made something are (probably) a better place to go for information. Wonder what I make? Visit bjmendelson.com for details.

13. Adam Carolla, podcast host and comedian, in discussion with the author, September 2011.

14. Michael Learmonth, "Why 500 Channels Means 19 Shows About Pawnshops," *Ad Age*, August 8, 2011. http://adage.com/article/media works/500-channels-means-19-shows-pawnshops/229153/

15. Cecilia Kang, "Comcast Yanks Funds for Nonprofit After Tweet About FCCs Baker's Jump," *The Washington Post*, May 19, 2011. http://www.washingtonpost.com/blogs/post-tech/post/comcast-yanks-funds-for-nonprofit-after-tweet-about-fcc-bakers-jump/2011/05/19/AF7aGG7G_blog.html

16. The "leaving money on the table" line came from Robert Scoble, king of the Cyber Hipsters. The full comment is as follows:

> The idea that we have a version for the Web is just plain ridiculous. It makes the innovations we're implementing too easily dismissed. How many times have you heard that "Twitter is lame?" I lost count 897 days ago.
>
> Now, is using a year number, like what I'm doing, better? Yes. It gets us out of the version lock. And it makes it clear to businesses that if you are still driving around a 1994 Web site that it's starting to look as old and crusty as a 1994 car is about now. Executives understand this. It's a rare executive who drives an old car around. Most like to have the latest expensive car to get to work in.
>
> Same with the Web. Calling it the "2010 Web" puts an ur-

gency into what's happening. If your business isn't considering the latest stuff it risks looking lame or, worse, leaving money on the table. Just like driving a 1994 car risks looking lame or, worse, breaking down a lot more often than a newer car."

For more, see: Robert Scoble, "Why Kara Swisher and Walt Mossberg Are Wrong About Naming Web 3.0 'Web 3.0,' *Scobleizer*, http://scobleizer.com/2009/05/29/kara-is-wrong-about-2010web/

17. Ben Popper, "Jack Dorsey Offers Mayor Bloomberg a Job at Twitter's First New York City Office," *Beta Beat*. October 6, 2011. http://www.betabeat.com/2011/10/06/jack-dorsey-offers-mayor-bloomberg-a-job-at-twitters-first-new-york-office/

18. You can see my car accident with Whet Moser, formerly of the *Chicago Reader*, here: http://www.chicagoreader.com/Bleader/archives/2009/09/17/tucker-max-fans-they-may-be-stupid-but-theyre-not-dweebs. I'd like to take this moment to apologize to Whet and the people at the Chicago Reader. I was an asshole. I apologize.

19. If anyone has a problem with this book, I encourage them to call me at 518-832-9844. If you leave me a voice-mail message with your e-mail address, or just e-mail me at bj@bjmendelson.com, I will write you back. I'm not a big phone guy, but you might just catch me if I'm in a chatty mood.

20. You can watch that *NBC Nightly News* interview with Mel Brooks here: http://www.bing.com/videos/watch/video/full-mel-brooks-interview/6ccsp0l?cpkey=9a31992b-48e9-42f6-86fa-3585afdfac5c%7C%7C%7C%7C